Essentials of Criminology

A Student-Oriented Approach to Teaching Crime Theory

Bassim Hamadeh, CEO and Publisher
Carrie Montoya, Manager, Revisions and Author Care
Kaela Martin, Project Editor
Christian Berk, Associate Production Editor
Jess Estrella, Senior Graphic Designer
Alexa Lucido, Licensing Associate
Natalie Piccotti, Senior Marketing Manager
Kassie Graves, Vice President of Editorial
Jamie Giganti, Director of Academic Publishing

Printed in the United States of America.

ISBN: 978-1-5165-3263-6 (pbk) / 978-1-5165-3264-3 (br)

Essentials of Criminology

A Student-Oriented Approach to Teaching Crime Theory

Second Edition

Lisa Coole

This edition is dedicated in loving memory of my father, Charles K. Austin (11/22/44–04/10/2018). He left this world earlier than our family was ready for, but he left behind an immeasurable fountain of wisdom for which I am eternally grateful.

Brief Contents

Detailed Contents

Chapter 3
Neo-Classical Theories 29

Chapter 4
Structure Theories 35

Chapter 5
Process Theories 47

Praise for *Essentials of Criminology*

Lisa Coole has provided an essential link between criminal justice (CJ) in practice and criminology in theory in this wonderful concise volume. For those of us teaching CJ, it is crucial to be able to connect the theoretical framework behind CJ policies to today's CJ practices and issues. Coole's book is unique in its easy-flowing reading format and transforms dry, dusty academic theories to life by providing both context and true-life experiences students can immediately relate to. This student-oriented approach lays the foundation necessary for the type of critical thinking tomorrow's CJ professional will find essential for success.

Aviva M. Rich-Shea, Ph.D., Associate Professor of Criminal Justice, Massasoit Community College

I thoroughly enjoyed Lisa's book. I found the format easy to follow and conversational. The book does not teach theory only, but asks students to draw upon their everyday knowledge and to challenge their perceptions. At the same time, they are also learning about crime theory. Unfortunately, the average citizen is bombarded with crime stories through news programs, websites, and television dramas. This is both productive and destructive for the classroom and for teaching crime theory. Students have emotions attached to particular discussions because they are familiar with certain crimes and are often willing to discuss their reactions. However, this can also hinder classroom discussion because a student's reaction can overshadow the content of the course. *Essentials of Criminology* takes these issues into account and provides discussion questions and activities in addition to examining the major theories associated with criminology. When I was reading the book, I felt like I was having an interactive conversation with Lisa Coole, the other possible students in the class, and the crime theorists of the past. This book is a wonderful addition to the classroom.

Dr. Rita Jones-Hyde, English Department, Massasoit Community College

Essentials of Criminology is an excellent book. It takes the essence of what every Criminology professor should teach and presents it logically and in an affordable package. This format allows the professor to customize their delivery without sacrificing the building blocks of criminology.

Patrick J. Faiella, Professor and Chair of the Criminal Justice Department at Massasoit Community College and President of the Massachusetts Association of Criminal Justice Education

Professor Coole truly excels at getting to the roots of the *Essentials of Criminology* without complex terminology that is not used in everyday life that we usually see in college level books. She uniquely educates the student to another extent, preparing you to use critical thinking from every aspect, but in a smooth, unintimidating manner. She offers realistic and personal experiences, relays raw factors, and gets to the point!

Fanuel Luna, former student

I certainly found it challenging at best to go from a practitioner of over 38 years back to theory and basic criminology text. Also, as a Director of State Corrections in Oklahoma where we are first per capita in the incarceration of adult females and third in adult males while continuing to experience yearly net offender growth, it was refreshing to travel back and read origins of sociological theory on criminality. Lisa's book was chronologically developed and presented in a logical and understandable manner.

Justin Jones, Director of the Oklahoma Department of Corrections

Lisa's *Essentials of Criminology* is a text that manages to simplify theory into accessible, personalized concepts, which would, in my opinion, make even the most reluctant students active participants in the dialogue the book creates.

The style of writing is a nice blend of academic and personal, which makes the book both less-menacing as a college textbook and more enjoyable for students to read. The information is presented casually but thoroughly, which I believe is the book's biggest strength. Criminology is far from my own field, but after reading *Essentials*, I realize that Lisa has successfully reached out across the curriculum to appeal to students (and faculty) with varying academic and personal interests. She achieves this by setting down real-world examples of concepts, linking common occurrences, such as drunk driving, smoking cigarettes, and cheating on exams, to the criminological theories she explains in the text.

Jared Gilpatrick, Adjunct Professor, Department of History & Government, Massasoit Community College

About the Author

Lisa C. Coole is a Tenured Associate Professor, with the Social Science Department at Massasoit Community College in Brockton and Canton, MA, and a Visiting Associate Professor at Bridgewater State University (formerly known as Bridgewater State College) in Bridgewater, MA. She received her bachelor's Degree in Sociology with a minor in Special Education and a concentration in Criminology from Bridgewater State College in 1989, and her master's Degree in Criminal Justice with a concentration in Criminology and Research from Northeastern University (Boston, MA) in 1991. She started her professorial career in 1993 at Trinity College in Burlington, VT, as adjunct faculty teaching undergraduate and graduate courses in Sociology and the Sociology of Law. Upon relocating to her native state of Massachusetts she resumed teaching as an adjunct lecturer at Bridgewater State College in 1998, where she continues to teach courses in both the Sociology and Criminal Justice Departments including Introductory Sociology, Criminology, Family and Intimate Relationships, Applied Crime Theory in Criminal Justice, Corrections, and Ethics in the Criminal Justice System. From 2001 to 2008 she was adjunct faculty at Stonehill College (Easton, MA) teaching primary Sociology, Criminology, and Corrections courses. As a current full-time member of the Social Science department at Massasoit Community College her courses include Introductory Sociology, Criminology, and Sociology of Deviance. Coole also served as her department's Chairperson from 2012–2014 during which time she launched a Social Science Transfer program. In addition to her teaching, Coole is involved in the professional development of her colleagues by facilitating workshops around issues of classroom protocol, civility, and inclusiveness. She also serves as an Academic Senator. Coole also has a passion for student advising and mentoring students regarding their careers and academic "next steps." In April 2018, she was the proud recipient of the Dean Marguerite A. Donovan Student Development Award in recognition of her outstanding contributions to the educational, social, and emotional development of students at Massasoit Community College.

Practitioner Background

In addition to various undergraduate and graduate internships, Coole has derived much of her "real-life" experience working directly in the criminal justice system. From 1988–1990 she worked as a Victim/Witness Advocate for the Massachusetts District Attorney's office. From 1991–2001 she was employed as a Federal Probation Officer for the District of Vermont and then the District of Massachusetts. She has also held part-time consulting and training positions for Community Resources for Justice, a privately run organization utilized by both state and federal correctional systems for prerelease programming.

Finally, in the words of her husband of 30 years, Coole is an "emotional philanthropist" to the many troubled souls along her long path in both her criminal justice and academic worlds. Her experiences in guiding and often redirecting their journeys have contributed greatly to her insight for her social science teaching, as well as this subject.

Acknowledgments

In 2002, I was asked to teach an introductory criminology course at Stonehill College in Easton, MA, as I was transitioning from my position as a federal probation officer to my career as a professor. While I had already been teaching adjunct courses in sociology and criminal justice, this was my first opportunity to be able to teach what I had exceptionally been taught at Northeastern University and Bridgewater State University and had practiced in various capacities of work in the criminal justice field. From that time forward, I was hooked on teaching this complex subject, and I am forever grateful for all my educators and mentors that made the inception possible, but especially Dr. Walter Carroll (undergraduate mentor) and the late Dr. Nicole Hahn Rafter (graduate mentor). Now, as a full-time faculty member at Massasoit Community College in Brockton, MA, and an adjunct faculty member at Bridgewater State University in Bridgewater, MA, I have been heavily engaged in teaching crime theories in various courses and course levels.

As I became more comfortable with the material, I found myself increasingly teaching from my professional and personal experiences to make the academic jargon "come alive." This had a noticeable positive impact on my students. In more recent years, students have consistently told me that they learn so much from my unique delivery. Students also advised that they found the assigned textbooks confusing and overwhelming. Unfortunately, though, when a student would miss a class, they were left to try to learn on their own from the text. But in reality, most would copy class notes from a fellow student as a much-preferred way to keep up with the class. So, when I was contacted by Cognella publishing to see if I would consider putting my teaching practices down on paper, I accepted, and I am most grateful for this opportunity.

In preparing to write this book, I first looked to my students, past and present, who were more than willing to lend me their honest feedback, criticisms, and class notes. From there I struggled initially in getting my course information, which primarily comes from my own head, into a written format. However, with the support of colleagues, family, and friends, I set out to pursue what I have since come to realize is uncharted territory.

Although so many students have had a positive impact on this project, I am especially grateful for Jessica Compston, Ruben Ortiz, Joshua Babineau, Robert Higginbotham, and Fanuel Luna (Massasoit Community College).

I am also grateful for the legal consulting assistance of Kara McCabe, Esq., in getting this project off the ground. Further, a special thank you to my sister Amy Austin Sheppard, LICSW, for putting me in touch with quality films and case studies though her own work in the field of juvenile delinquency intervention.

For this second edition, I returned to a recent stellar student from Massasoit Community College, Jared Marshall, for his wisdom. I am very grateful to Jared, who lent his expertise in researching topics, updating statistics, reviewing theories, and contributing his own insights from having taken this course at the Honor's level. Jared is now pursuing his sociology degree with a concentration in crime and justice and a minor in history at Suffolk University in Boston, MA. As an honors student in this program, I have no doubt that his pursuit of law school will be achieved.

I am deeply in debt to my husband, Garry, who helped with much of the editing and proofing for the first edition, but most importantly encouraged me to keep moving forward and not give up. I am also thankful to my parents, Charles and Linda Austin, who supported my higher education pursuits and instilled a work ethic and attitude that I rely on heavily. Finally, I am thankful to my two children, Austin and Amy, as I am sure having a mommy who was working with criminals for much of their childhood was not always easy.

New to This Edition

Welcome to the second edition of what has turned out to be a great addition to teaching this subject in both 2- and 4-year college systems. The feedback from the first edition, which I have been using for more than five years, with an average of 75 students per semester, has been most favorable. Students have expressed appreciating the cost, relevance, and practicality of the text as opposed to a traditional criminology textbook. Colleagues using the text have especially appreciated suggested activities and assignments. As for myself, I have also found the text useful in reducing the amount of time needed to reexplain concepts when students miss class or are struggling with the pace of the class, as the text mirrors the key points needed for learning and eventual assessment of their comprehension. Although nothing can replace the class lectures and discussions that go beyond what is in print, this text is an integral part of a student's academic tool kit. Additionally, our department added a social science transfer degree, which has brought more and more noncriminal justice students in to the classroom. Many of these students are undecided about a specific major, but know they have a desire to work around human behavior and/or policy and recognize how understanding crime and delinquency enhances their knowledge and future endeavors (i.e., medicine, substance abuse counseling, education, politics, etc.). The changes to the second edition recognize the need to connect with this larger audience by expanding criminal justice core concepts in Chapter 1, additional theories in Chapter 5, and additional examples, activities and assignments. The table of contents also now identifies key topics, terminologies, and the names of specific theories and subcategories for an easy first glance of what each chapter entails.

In the spirit of debunking as many myths as possible, statistical data highlighted in the opening chapter has been updated to reflect the most recent reports. Finally, in this time of social change and tensions surrounding, but not limited to, police-community relations, immigration policy, sexual misconduct, mass shootings, and gun control I have incorporated these themes throughout the text's examples, activities, and assignments.

Preface

I have been teaching the subject matter of criminology, also referred to as crime theory, over fifteen years to a wide variety of students in a variety of college settings. While most recently my instruction has been based at an urban community college and a four-year state school, I have found a few common obstacles in all venues that hinder student successes. Given my firm belief that the best educators are willing and able to reassess their instruction methods and to use their students as a major gauge of success (aka: classroom research), I decided a few years back to really embrace the mission of classroom research for both my introductory and upper level crime theory courses. The results of meeting with students, combing over their class notes, having casual discussions with colleagues, facilitating classroom research workshops with faculty, and revising my course delivery led me to the realization that there are several common mindsets that hinder student success. Of the more prevalent issues observed, the most persistent student concerns are:

- What is the point in having to take a course like this, especially as a criminal justice major?
- Why are there so many categories of theory?
- Why does the text use terminologies that don't make sense to me?
- I don't see myself ever using this "stuff" in a real-world setting.
- Why do I find myself relating to and enjoying the material in class, yet being unable to retain and express what I have learned on exams?

One of the more surprising discoveries I made during my classroom research and assessment was that many of my successful students admittedly were not using the textbook assigned for the course. Some stated it was due to the high cost of textbooks, but even when given the option to rent or borrow, consistent feedback regarding the text was that it was overwhelming and counterproductive to their success in learning and comprehending the material. While I believe that my current pedagogy deserves credit for student success in my courses, there is always room for improvement, and there is more than one way to teach this subject matter. My hope and objective in writing this text is to provide students, and perhaps other colleagues, with a tool that will assist them as an ancillary to my methods in the classroom. I have also found that today's students are more distracted than ever. Whether the distractions are caused by the outside influences of social media, juggling work and/or family life or the more proximate factors such as learning disabilities, emotional struggles, and other challenges, having a hands-on text will be a valued asset.

My courses are lecture-based in format and supplemented by student-led discussions, documentary case study reviews, scholarly research assignments, and, depending on the course level, a project and/or presentation. My delivery is not fancy and does not utilize some of the common resources in this age of technology (i.e. PowerPoint presentations, online instruction). Student assessments are appropriately frequent for my student population, utilizing objective and subjective testing, outside research, critical thinking writing assignments, and a cumulative final examination. I am opposed to high-stakes examination and assessment; therefore, all measurements carry the same worth towards the final course grade calculation.

While this text has been tailored to fit my course(s), I would encourage anyone who is struggling to reach today's student to consider this text. It is a unique approach and purposefully will be unlike other traditional theory texts. While I respect all of those who have written and edited great texts and anthologies in this field, I am both intrigued by and thankful for this opportunity to put my teaching practices into print and to see how this somewhat radical approach to a text on criminological theory will assist students in better achieving their professional and educational goals.

About the Text Format

This resource is designed as a primary text for any course striving to engage students in learning about criminological theory. The text is centered around Edwin Sutherland's (1978) complete definition of criminology, aka: crime theory, which is the study of law makers, law breakers, and societal reactions to law breakers. This text will be especially useful in today's climate of ever-changing departmental objectives, in which many schools aim to teach crime theory as an applied science.

This text is written in a non-conventional, informal format intended to better reach students in a real, practical, and most importantly memorable fashion without compromising the integrity of this academic field. For this I am thankful to the many authors, theorists, and researchers who have contributed to this complex field and created the information I have devoured. Their work makes it possible for me to deliver in this fashion.

The chapter layout is designed to ease students into the subject matter by establishing some core concepts essential to appreciating the theoretical components. Subsequent chapters are organized around theories that shape a common thread so that students may appreciate the necessity to aggregate theories. Additionally, activities and reflections are also suggested within the chapters, which could be used as in-class or homework assignments. More significant assignments are included in the final chapter of the text to help students understand the daunting task of theory in practice.

For the sake of more profound learning, a selected group of theories are illustrated so that students may have a well-rounded foundation. Brief mention or simple references to other theories are made for those who wish to continue their exploration of the myriad of theories in this field. Finally, this text has as its central theme keeping students interested and on track with discussions that address the previously mentioned mindset obstacles.

Chapter 1

Why Study Crime Theory?

Success in college often depends on how well you are invested in a course. Many students taking this course are doing so to complete a degree requirement for a program of study. Some have chosen it as an elective. Few have a strong desire to learn about theory, and many are dreading having to take a "theory" course. My intent is to get you excited about this course regardless of your initial reason for taking it. I suggest you take a minute and reflect on the following questions:

- Have you ever watched a news story or other form of mass media about criminal behavior and wondered, "Why would anyone do such a thing?"
- Have you ever been the victim of a crime and had it affect you, financially, physically, or psychologically?
- Have you ever been accused and/or convicted of a crime and wondered how it will affect your future personal, academic, or professional endeavors?
- Are you aware that the criminal justice system operates primarily on our tax dollars?
- Do you know how to assess the extent and nature of criminal behavior in any given demographic area?
- Do you plan on working in the criminal justice system or a related field?

Although the list of reasons that justify learning about crime theory is endless, hopefully the above questions will make you feel confident that your time will not be wasted in taking this course.

What Is Criminology?

Depending on your institution, the course you are taking likely involves the terms criminology or crime theory. These terms are interchangeable, and both may be defined as the systematic and scientific study of crime and specifically, the three major areas needed to fully analyze crime in our society:

- Law breakers
- Law makers
- Societal reaction to law breakers

The above definition was introduced by Edwin Sutherland (1978) and goes beyond the simple definition of the study of crime. The reason for doing so is to appreciate the complexity of criminal behavior and to see how the relationship between our law makers and our societal reactions impacts our understanding of criminal behaviors. For example, if the laws changed to make "tagging" and other forms of graffiti art legal, imagine the impact this would have on society. Individuals once considered delinquent and criminal may now be artists. On the contrary, if the law changed to make it a criminal offense to come to class late, how would that impact the overall college experience? Although extreme, these examples also elicit follow-up questions such as: Would people still complain about graffiti? Would dropout rates of students increase or decrease? The responses to these questions are complex and depend in part on what we think about why people do graffiti in the first place or why students are late to class. Also, as with any law that is created, to what extent it will be enforced and what the punishments would be are legitimate concerns.

Where to Start?

Although the complete definition of criminology is necessary, and each element of criminology will be examined during this course, at this early stage, the following statement provides a good place to start the inquiry process. Once understood, it should fuel a desire (no matter how small) to want to advance in this course. Take a moment to read the following statement and reflect on how it makes you feel.

"What people think about why YOU do certain things impacts how they react to YOU when they observe or hear about your behavior." (Coole, 2012)

We can all relate to a time in our life when we have been misunderstood or someone has (in our view at least) overreacted to something that we may have said or done. Often, we think, they don't understand, or they have the wrong idea. I can remember the first time my daughter had a temper tantrum as a teenager. I also remember how my reaction to her tantrum was influenced by my understanding of the series of events she had going on in her social and academic life that had her extremely on edge and sensitive. While her behavior was not ignored, the response was considerate of the social forces that influenced her behavior.

So where is all this going, and what does this have to do with studying crime theory? The criminal justice system has been charged with the awesome function of investigating, apprehending, processing, and punishing criminals. The major components of the system, law enforcement, courts, and corrections (both institutional and community) play unique roles in reaching various aims. In other words, the criminal justice system is in the "reacting business." Although it is common knowledge that the system does not work as cohesively and effectively as society might expect, if we are to criticize what is not working, advocate for what is working, and/or suggest alternatives that might work better, it would only make sense that we recommend policies and practices that are theoretically sound, as opposed to suggestions that are socially and/or politically charged.

It is a known fact that the corporal punishment of children (i.e., spanking) is ineffective and in many cases harmful in the development of a child. Why, then, do some parents continue to spank their children? The same goes for dealing with criminals: whether it be at the informal level, as parents and teachers, or at the formal levels of criminal justice authority, there are preventive and reactive measures taken that are done in the name of tradition and/or antiquated practices that have proven ineffective. Hence, the ultimate goal of the criminal justice system and the government institutions that effect legal changes and policy should aim for effective outcomes, and at the very least, avoidance of negative outcomes, such as not reducing crime and/or recidivism.

The Criminal Justice System

Who exactly is responsible for achieving effective outcomes as noted above? As noted above, the criminal justice is comprised of three essential components, **law enforcement**, **courts**, and **corrections**. Within each component are the individuals and agencies at the federal, state, and local levels given the authority to achieve their goals within the constraints of the professional ethics and standards governing their duties. Whether it be a police officer's protocol when responding to a domestic violence call, a prosecutor decision on whether to press, drop, or amend charges for a first-time shoplifter, a judge's rule at sentencing, or the recommendation of a probation or parole officer regarding bail, violations of conditions, or adjusting conditions of release—these individuals, along with many others, all play a part in the criminal justice system.

One important aspect to the work of those within the system to keep in mind, however, is that not everyone has the same ideas as about achieving their tasks in terms of the ultimate goals and the process by which to achieve them. Students pursuing criminal justice and related degrees will no doubt spend time examining these goals and mechanisms in detail. However, as students of theory, familiarity with the premises of the two main models of the criminal justice system, **Crime Control** and **Due Process**, as well as an overview of the criminal justice process will no doubt aid in theory comprehension and application.

Crime Control versus Due Process

In 1968, Herbert Packer, a Stanford University law professor, constructed these two models of the criminal justice system. As you read through a summary of the highlighted differences and objectives of the two, you should see clearly why we have conflicts and controversy in our society in terms of addressing and controlling crime. And as will be explored further in the next chapter, both have their merits, yet they reflect different values, concerns, and priorities, making consensus difficult, if not impossible to achieve.

Crime Control	Due Process
The most important function of the criminal justice system (CJS) is to repress crime so that society may be protected and remain free.	The most important function of the CJS is to provide due process of law, protecting all from unfair treatment by the government.
Resources should be prioritized toward the vindication of victims' and their families over protecting the defendant's rights is essential.	The Bill of Rights supports that the defendant's rights are given priority over the victim's rights.
Expanding law enforcement powers should be a priority in order to make investigations, arrests, and convictions easier.	Law enforcement power should be limited to prevent official oppression of individuals.
The CJS process should move as swiftly as to bring speedy justice; it should operate like an assembly line.	The CJS process should move carefully to avoid mistakes and violation of civil rights; it should operate like an obstacle course.
It is reasonable to assume that the accused is guilty because the police and prosecutors are reliable fact-finders.	It is essential to protect the innocent and hold the government to its burden of proof and legal standard of innocent until proven guilty.

Activity/Reflection: Consider the following quote by Packer (1964) and whether it reflects the crime control or due process model? Also, what current legal debates do these views add insight?

> "... maximal efficiency means maximal tyranny." (p. 3)

The Criminal Justice Process

What does the journey look like for the law breakers? Do all offenders have the same chance of being caught up in the system, and moreover, do they experience the same encounters along the way? It is critical to understand that the answer to this question is a resounding NO! There are many stages to this complex process as seen in the chart below depicting various points of entry *and* departure. An analogy I have found useful to help students understand and appreciate the criminal justice process and procedure is a sand sifter. Imagine the shore of a beach and that each grain of sand, pebble, or rock represents individuals committing crime and that the sand sifter is the criminal justice system. Will the sifter catch every grain of sand, pebble, or rock? Undoubtedly not only will many grains never make it into the sifter, but if you were to shake the sifter for even just a few seconds, what remains does not reflect what you started with. Why this mirrors the criminal justice process does not have a simple answer. Some of the contributing factors will be discussed later in this text and course, however, acknowledging that the criminal justice system has holes like a sand sifter is essential to appreciating many of the theories.

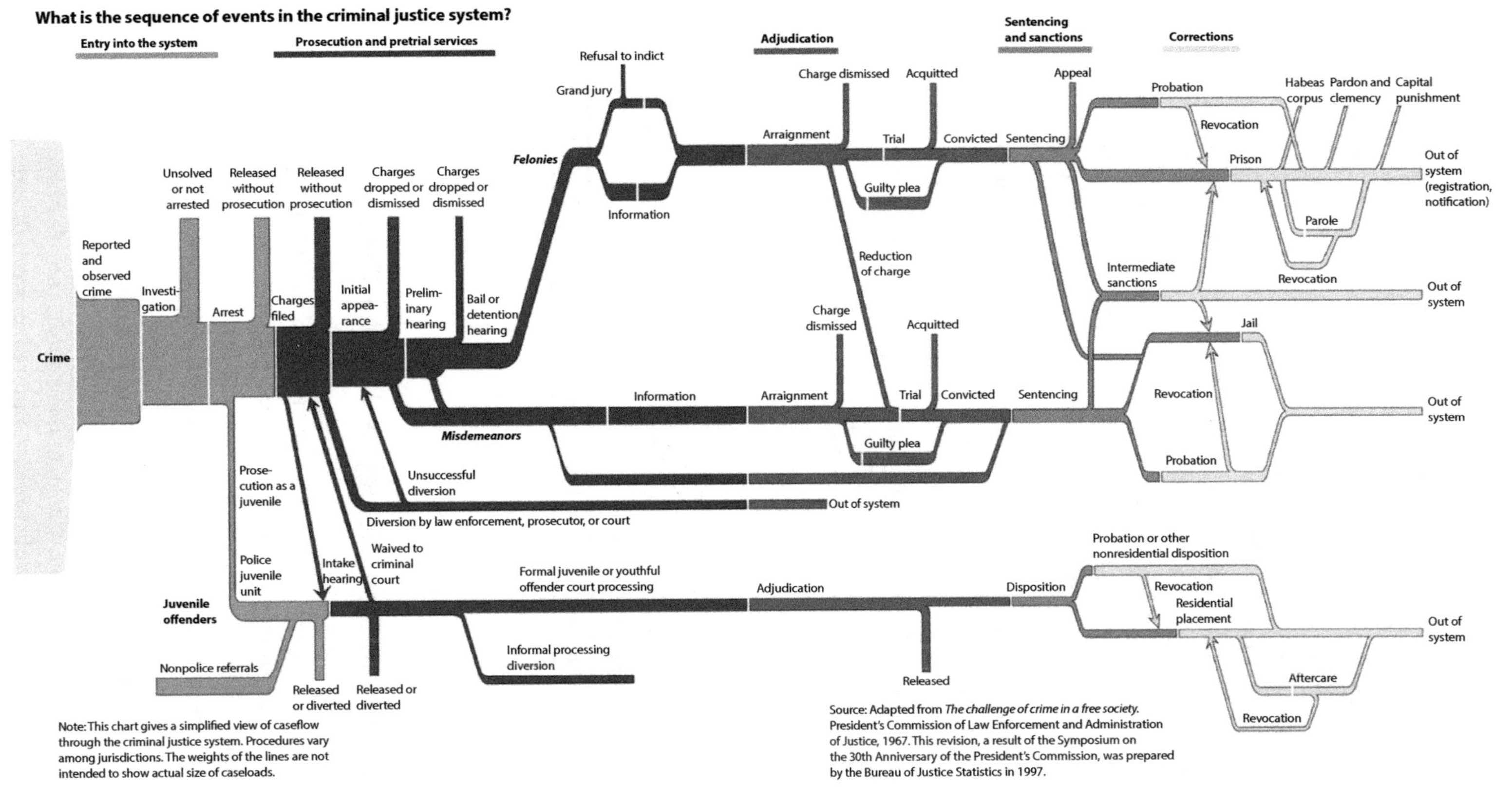

Figure 1.1 What is the sequence of events in the criminal justice system?

Activity: Before moving forward with theory, students should have a basic level of understanding about how some of the "players" on the "team" of criminal justice play a role in various aspects of criminal behavior. The following activity could be done in small groups or as a take home assignment. In-class discussion may also stimulate a desire to learn more and validate this academic field.

For each of the three main components of the criminal justice system, identify three distinct job titles and note briefly to what extent these main components play a role in crime prevention, apprehension of law breakers, sentencing of the convicted, correctional supervision, and offender reintegration. Students should be able to see how many of the players in the system are involved in more than one area. For example, while many people assume that a probation officer plays a role in community correctional supervision, they may not realize that probation officers also have a significant part in the sentencing process. Probation officers also work with law enforcement when a violation has occurred to ensure community safety and enforcement of conditions that might require discretionary decisions about consequences for behavior.

Step 1. Identify three distinct job functions/job titles for each component.

Law Enforcement	Courts	Corrections

Step 2. Briefly note how at least two of the three main components play a role for each of the four aspects of crime reduction.

Crime Prevention	Apprehension of Offenders	Sentencing	Correctional Supervision

The Academics of Criminology and Crime Theory

Concerns over why criminals, or anyone for that matter, do the things they do is nothing recent. Since the beginning of time societies have pondered such. As society has evolved, the level of inquiry has become more sophisticated and scientific. No longer are we content to blame deviance, whether it be criminal or not, on demon-filled spirits or a full moon. While we certainly regard some of the most horrific crimes, such as the orchestrations of serial killers, child rapists, and terrorists, as perhaps being aligned with "pure evil," we understand that human beings and their behaviors are more complex. The academic field of sociology, which relies heavily on understanding the role of social forces, has been the driving force behind many of the most admired, criticized, and applicable theories.

Also contributing to this inquiry are the fields of psychology and biology. More recently, students pursuing degrees in other fields such as politics, education, social justice, and human services, also benefit from having theories on crime and deviance integrated within their domains of study.

Due to time restraints, and in the interest of staying on task with theories that are the most feasible, this text will examine theories developed primarily from and within a sociological context. For this reason, it is important that students generally appreciate the differences between and among the three main academic fields' inquiries into human behavior, whether it be criminal or not.

Biological theories focus on genetics, physical features, and physiological factors. **Psychological** theories focus on individual factors (derived from nature and/or nurture) involving the mind and the development of personality and character through the life span. Consideration is also given to the impact of traumatic events and mental disorders. Both fields are extremely complex and worthy of consideration, and students are encouraged to explore fundamental courses in these areas. However, when it comes to explaining criminal behavior and the related issues, these theories for the most part have not been incorporated due to a lack of supporting evidence and/or unrealistic, costly, and unethical implementation strategies.

Grinch Analogy

Over the years, I have received favorable response with an analogy I developed that incorporates Dr. Seuss's *The Grinch Who Stole Christmas* to help illustrate the general differences in the biological, psychological, and sociological approach to explaining the Grinch's criminality. After all, he is a burglar. This story has been illustrated in a children's book, a cartoon, and more recently, a film starring Jim Carrey entitled *The Grinch*. If asked why the Grinch was a criminal according to the original book, one may draw the conclusion that because his heart was "two sizes too small" he was physically unable to be empathetic. This exemplifies a biological approach. To fix his criminal ways, a surgical procedure should do the job. In the cartoon, his malady is elaborated a bit more, and one might conclude that it had an impact on his thought process and that he was consumed with greed and jealousy. This exemplifies his physiological disorder impacting his emotions and personality. This is a more psychological level of inquiry. However, through the last film, *The Grinch*, we are given a deeper insight that elaborates on what might be the root causes and suggests that they come from his upbringing, which included being bullied by his peers for being different, being raised in an unconventional family setting, being jilted by his childhood crush, and living in a filthy and alienated living space as an adult. These factors are more **sociological** in nature and will be essential components of the theories taught throughout this course.

The sociological approach to studying crime in hopes of gaining insight, explanation, and application relies heavily on the role of outside social forces and institutions such as family, peers, school, mass media, religion, and politics. Students in this course should have a foundation in the essential principles of sociological perspectives and concepts.

Terminology Refresher

As a refresher, I have developed a brief bank of terms that students should review and be prepared to discuss in class:

Sociological Imagination: Recognizing that thoughts and behavior are affected by where we are historically, culturally, and politically, as well as the immediate social forces that shape our thoughts and behaviors (Mills, 1959).

Subjective Interpretation: Appreciating that as humans we attach meaning to symbols, which can be anything from a piece of clothing to music, a facial expression, or even a tone of voice. What is most important to understand is that there is no universal meaning for any symbol. In other words, the meaning we attach to a symbol is subject to our own interpretation and can change from one setting to the next.

Norms: Norms are the formal and informal social rules in society that help us understand different cultures and societies. Most students learn about norms in an introductory level sociology course. There are three types of norms: folkways, mores, and laws. Folkways are weaker norms, and mores are more culturally embedded and will likely get a stronger reaction when violated. Laws are those norms that have been written into law and are part of our criminal justice system. This course focuses on law norms; however, recognizing the influence of other types of norms will be very much appreciated and incorporated.

Values: Values are the underlying set of beliefs about what is right or good that are often reflected through norms. However, there is no exact equation by which to match norms with precise values. Values and norms are also subject to interpretation. For example, a student who comes in late to class on the first day is clearly violating the norm for a college student. To one professor, this may reflect a value of disrespect and irresponsibility. Yet, to another professor, it might indicate dedication and responsibility, as the student is willing to violate this social norm and risk being looked at or even scolded. To this person, the value to getting an education, even if coming in late, is worth the risk. But again, the interpretation of this behavior lies in the eyes of the perceiver—in this case, the professor.

Subculture: Simply defined, a subculture is a culture within a larger culture. Individuals who are part of a subculture will share many parts of their culture (knowledge, beliefs, behaviors, values, symbolisms) with the mainstream culture they are part of.

Status: A status may be defined as one's position in society. Normally, people associate this word with wealth or someone of high regard. Sociologically, this term is used to identify the various statuses that we hold that may be either ascribed (such as race or gender) or achieved (such as being a student or parent).

Socialization: The concept of socialization should be familiar to students taking a course in crime theory through previous coursework in sociology and psychology. Socialization is a process word that helps explain how we become the type of people we are regarding our character, personality, and other traits. Socialization recognizes that nurture is alive in this process. The active role of the four main agents of socialization—family, schools, peers, and media (mass and social)—as well other agents such as religion, politics, and community, are key. One way to think about socialization is to try to understand certain qualities, behaviors, and attitudes in others by asking who is to blame or deserves credit. For example, "What is wrong with that person?" or "What kind of parents did they have?" or "I wonder if being obsessed with video games, reality television, or horror movies impacts behavior?" These questions are birthed out of socialization. The process of socialization looks at how we learn to think, express our feelings and emotions, keep in line with the normal rules of society, and develop our sense of morality and social maturity. Although this subject matter alone is worth several class discussions, it is a theme that will be brought into many theoretical discussions in this course.

Research Methods

Many of you have thoughts as to why crime exists in our society, the impact of our laws, and/or to what extent the criminal justice system is working. Some of your ideas may come from personal experience as an offender or victim, or having a close friend or family member involved in the system. For some, your ideas are based on television shows, social media, news accounts, or even the big screen. Perhaps you currently work in the criminal justice system or know someone who does. The reality is that there are many sources that play a role in forming your opinions. This knowledge, which is commonly referred to as **conventional knowledge**, is part of the human condition, especially in a society with vast, yet in many ways grotesque, access to information. But as students pursuing academic knowledge, you must be able to admit that this type of knowledge is flawed. This is mainly because of the primary sources of conventional knowledge—*personal experiences*, what we have been told by others who we perceive to have *authority* on a subject matter, and *traditional viewpoints* that exist in the unique dynamics of our lives.

We have all found ourselves being asked for our opinions, whether it be from a friend in need of advice, engaging in a lively political discussion, or in our own thoughts as we ponder why people are the way they are. My bet is that we rarely, if ever, attempt to confirm or rebut our viewpoints with research-based evidence.

One does not need to conduct elaborate studies and research to have access to information that goes beyond conventional knowledge. There are many individuals who dedicate much of their professional energy to attempting to prove or disprove information that we can use in our own assessments.

A **hypothesis** is an educated guess about a relationship among a set of testable principles attempting to explain any given issue in society, whether it be a cure for disease, a healthier way to make fast food, or a way to reduce crime. Social scientists use a variety of research methods to test their hypotheses in hopes of establishing proven relationships among variables that may be tested and ultimately used as a plausible answer, or "cure." For this text and course, there will be an assumption that students have a general familiarity with the major research methods used in the social sciences, as well as with the strengths and shortcomings of the methods in terms of validity and ethical considerations. Listed below are some of the more common types of research methods:

- Surveys
- Observations
- Ethnographies
- Experiments
- Analyses of existing data
- Case studies
- Longitudinal studies
- Cohort studies

The objective of this text and course is to focus on theories. There is an overwhelming amount of research in this field, but this text will provide students with a more rigorous examination of essential theories. Some research has resulted in critique, leading to further theory development and/or revisions and modification. What should be kept in mind is that there are no perfect explanations, and many theories are purposefully limited in scope, yet still worthy of review. Questioning theory is encouraged in examining the various explanations for such complex matter; however, it is important to not hold a theory accountable for behaviors that a particular theory may not be focused on. In other words, don't expect to have the best cheeseburger in the world from a Thai food restaurant. But the Pad Thai should be pretty decent. Get it?

It is also important to know how to locate research, most of which is in scholarly journals found in collegiate institutions' library databases. Assignments may be given that will require you to locate, read, and analyze this type of research to meet course objectives. A primary objective for any such assignment is to ensure that you appreciate the caution of drawing conclusions on criminal justice matters based solely on nonscholarly resources such as newspapers, Internet searches, blogs, magazines, and even your own conventional knowledge.

Sources of Crime Data

Crime is often used to measure how healthy a society is. If society is viewed like a human, then crime might be morbid obesity, a fever, or cancer. In other words, a community or part of the country that has a low crime rate, especially violent crime, may indicate that this area is doing well economically and socially. Conversely, we tend to draw negative conclusions about the economic, familial, and education systems in communities with high crime rates. And as will be seen, finding answers to crime is as necessary as finding answers to the above afflictions. The problem is that it is far easier to get somewhat accurate accounts on cancer victims than on crime victims or offenders. But even with physical health, it is impossible to truly capture statistics on the various ailments with certainty and 100% accuracy.

When my husband and I decided to move to a suburb in Massachusetts, we looked for a community that would be a good place to raise our two children. Of the many considerations one has in settling down and raising a family, we were fortunate enough to be able to consider safety and crime issues (recognizing that not everyone can choose where they live). For this reason, we opted out of moving to the nearby city of Brockton, MA, which had a reputation of violent crime, drugs, and gang activity. Despite our efforts to protect our children from crime, by his freshman year in high school my son had witnessed a traumatizing, brutal, bloody attack at his suburban high school. Off- and on-campus fights continue to be all too common, and our community has lost far too many young people to suicide, drug overdoses, and violence. But wait—how could this happen in a supposedly safe community? No community is "safe." We should be wise to the fact that how crimes are portrayed, reported, and sensationalized in certain communities leads to inaccurate conclusions.

Crime is difficult to measure, yet it is necessary to measure it as accurately as possible. This task is complicated by bias and discretion in apprehending and reporting crime, whether it be by law enforcement, victims, or witnesses. Regardless, awareness of the main resources used currently to measure crime and their unique differences, advantages, and shortcomings is essential. The graph below shows that there is a disconnect between public perception and the reality of crime.

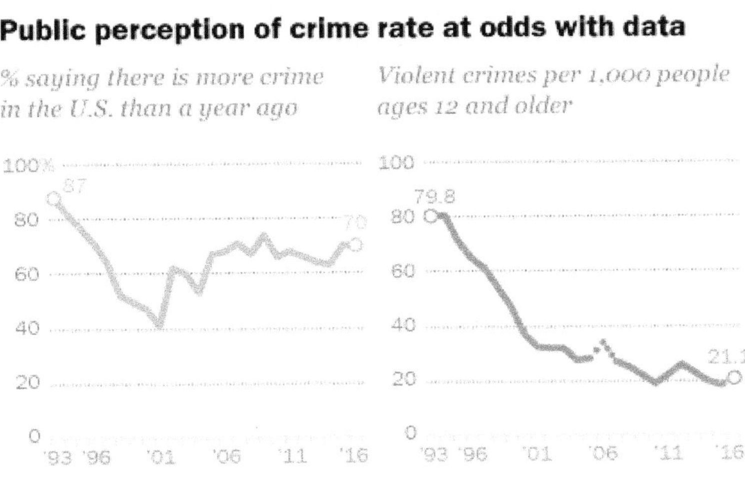

Figure 1.2 Public Perception of Crime Rate at Odds with Data.

Main Sources of Crime Data

Uniform Crime Report and the National Incident Based Reporting System

The above two data collection systems rely on information provided by law enforcement upon arrest. This information is voluntary but is used by a majority of agencies throughout the country. The Uniform Crime Report (UCR) is maintained by the Federal Bureau of Investigation (FBI), but information is derived from all levels (federal, state, local) of law enforcement. The UCR has been amended and eventually will be replaced by the National Incident Based Reporting System (NIBRS). NIBRS provides more detailed and comprehensive information and addresses some of the concerns associated with relying on police data and the collection methods of the FBI, which initially only looked at the most serious charge in multicharge arrests and the most serious types of crime.

Consider to what degree the information compiled by these sources challenges your preconceived notions about certain aspects of crime.

National Crime Victimization Survey

As part of the victims' rights movement in the United States during the 1970s, attention was given to the realization that relying on police data as the only source of crime information is severely flawed and ignorant. The National Crime Victimization Survey (NCVS) was developed to look specifically at those crimes that are routinely underreported by victims. It also addressed the fact that police discretion contributes to underreported data. The NCVS brings greater awareness to crimes such as domestic violence and sexual crimes, which are commonly underreported, and also property and economic crimes such as embezzlement, fraud, and burglary, which have surprisingly low reporting rates as well.

The following highlights from a recent report from the U.S. Bureau of Justice Statistics (BJS) exemplifies the need to have multiple sources to understand the reality of crimes:

Highlights include the following:

- The number of serious violent crimes not reported to the police increased from 42% in 2010 to 48.7% in 2016.
- In 2016, the highest percentages of unreported crime were among rape or sexual assault (77.1%) and theft (70.3%), whereas the lowest percentage was among motor vehicle theft (20.1%) victimizations. These are the same crimes that were reported from 2006–2010, but the percentages have increased, and more rapes have gone unreported compared with thefts.
- In 2016, violence committed by a stranger (55.3%) went unreported to the police, compared with domestic violence (50.9%).
- Unlike the period from 2006–2010, violence committed by a stranger was unreported more often to the police in 2016 than domestic violence, rather than vice versa.

- In 2016, violence committed by a stranger had a higher percentage of unreported incidents compared with 2006–2010, whereas domestic violence had a lower percentage of unreported incidents compared with 2006–2010.

TABLE 1.1 Relationship of Victims to Offenders by Offense Category, 2016.*

		Relationship of Victims to Offenders				
Offense Category	**Total Victims[1]**	**Family Member[2]**	**Family Member and Other[3]**	**Known to Victim and Other[4]**	**Stranger**	**All Other[5]**
Total	**1,394,512**	**298,274**	**40,281**	**730,882**	**145,250**	**179,825**
Crimes Against Persons	**1,323,972**	**297,628**	**40,076**	**716,513**	**116,581**	**153,174**
Assault Offenses	**1,218,338**	271,940	39,088	659,905	108,674	138,731
Homicide Offenses	**4,522**	652	43	1,764	526	1,537
Human Trafficking Offenses	**202**	4	4	130	22	42
Kidnapping/Abduction	**17,844**	3,787	205	9,922	1,672	2,258
Sex Offenses	**78,040**	20,128	668	41,427	5,591	10,226
Sex Offenses, Nonforcible	**5,026**	1,117	68	3,365	96	380
Crimes Against Property	**70,540**	**646**	**205**	**14,369**	**28,669**	**26,651**
Robbery	**70,540**	646	205	14,369	28,669	26,651

[1]The relationship of a victim to an offender is reported only for the victim types of Individual and Law Enforcement Officer that are connected to Crimes Against Persons or Robbery offenses. Relationship data are not collected for victims of offenses reported with an unknown offender or of other Crimes Against Property or Crimes Against Society offenses.
[2]Victims were related to all offenders, whether one or more, of the reported offense.
[3]Victims were related to at least one of the multiple offenders of the reported offense.
[4]Victims knew, but were not related to, one or more of the multiple offenders of the reported offense.
[5]Victims were mutual combatants (victim was offender) or had an unknown relationship with a single offender. In the case of multiple offenders, victims' relationships were combinations of strangers, mutual combatants, and/or unknown offenders.

---

* Table 1.1 Note: Counts are rounded to the nearest 100 and include estimates for nonresponding jurisdictions. Detail may not sum to total due to rounding and because offenders with dual correctional statuses were excluded from the total correctional population but included in individual populations. See Methodology.: Not calculated. [a]To avoid double counting, the total represents the combined probation, prison, parole, and jail counts minus those who have dual correctional statuses. See Methodology. [b]Population as of December 31. [c]Population as of the last weekday in June. [d]Some probationers and parolees on December 31 were held in a prison or jail but still remained under the jurisdiction of a probation or parole agency, and some parolees were also on probation. In addition, some prisoners were being held in jail. See table 5 and Methodology. Source: Bureau of Justice Statistics (BJS), Annual Probation Survey, Annual Parole Survey, Annual Survey of Jails, and National Prisoner Statistics program, 2007 and 2016.

TABLE 1.2 Murder and Nonnegligent Manslaughter and Aggravated Assault Victims Offense Type by Circumstance, 2016*[1].

		Offense Type	
Circumstance	Total Victims	Murder and Nonnegligent Manslaughter	Aggravated Assault
Argument	**112,983**	935	112,048
Assault on Law Enforcement Officer	**6,955**	39	6,916
Drug Dealing	**1,536**	201	1,335
Gangland Killing (Organized Crime)	**936**	42	894
Juvenile Gang (Street Gang)	**528**	11	517
Lovers' Quarrel	**15,534**	162	15,372
Mercy Killing[2]	**9**	9	
Other Felony Involved	**2,813**	125	2,688
Other Circumstances	**47,659**	881	46,778
Unknown Circumstances	**52,030**	2,360	49,670

[1]This table does not include a total row because a victim can be connected to up to two circumstances describing the murder and nonnegligent manslaughter or aggravated assault.
[2]The circumstance of mercy killing is not applicable to aggravated assault.

* Note: Rates are estimated to the nearest 10. Estimates may not be comparable with previously published BJS reports due to updated information or rounding. See the Key Statistics page on the BJS website for correctional population statistics prior to 2000 or other years excluded in this table. [a]Includes offenders in the community under the authority of probation or parole agencies, under the jurisdiction of state or federal prisons, or in the custody of local jails. [b]Includes offenders under the jurisdiction of state or federal prisons or held in local jails. [c]Rates are based on U.S. Census Bureau estimates of the U.S. resident population, age eighteen or older, for January 1 of the following year. [d]Rates are based on U.S. Census Bureau estimates of the U.S. resident population, all ages, for January 1 of the following year. Source: Bureau of Justice Statistics (BJS), Annual Probation Survey, Annual Parole Survey, Annual Survey of Jails, and National Prisoner Statistics program, 2000 and 2006–2016; and U.S. Census Bureau, postcensal resident populations for January of the following year 2001 and 2006–2016.

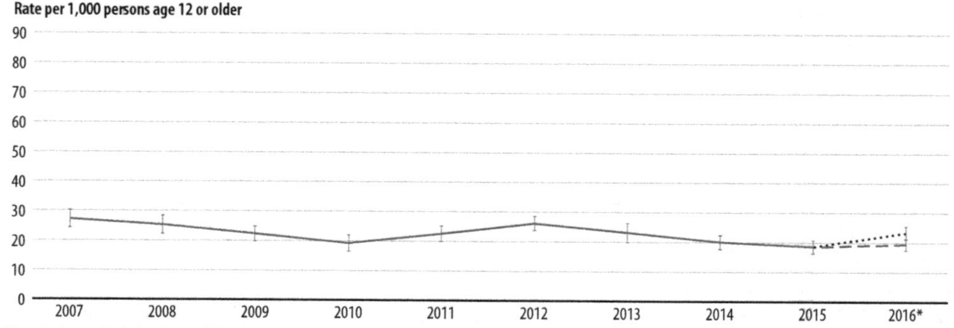

Note: Estimates include 95% confidence intervals. See appendix table 3 for estimates and standard errors.

*Dashed line for 2016 includes continuing sample counties only. Dotted line for 2016 includes new sample counties only and is for illustration only. See *Methodology* for more information on changes in the 2016 NCVS.

Source: Bureau of Justice Statistics, National Crime Victimization Survey (NCVS), 2007–2016; and U.S. Census Bureau, National Crime Victimization Survey Internal Data, 2016.

Figure 1.3 Violent victimization, 2007–2016.

TABLE 1.3 Rate of crime reported to police in the Uniform Crime Reporting Program and National Crime Victimization Survey, 2016.

Type of Crime	UCR Rate per 1,000 Residents[a]	NCVS Rate per 1,000 Persons Age 12 or Older
Serious violent crime[b]	3.9	3.6
Murder	0.1	~
Rape[c]	0.4	0.3
Robbery	1.0	1.0
Aggravated assault	2.5	2.3
	UCR Rate per 1,000 Residents[a]	**NCVS Rate per 1,000 Households**
Property Crime	24.5	42.6
Burglary	4.7	12.3
Motor vehicle theft	2.4	3.5

Note: See appendix table 7 for standard errors.
~Not applicable.
[a]Includes crimes against persons age 12 or younger, persons who are homeless, persons who are institutionalized, and crimes against commercial establishments. These populations are out of sample for the NCVS.
[b]In addition to rape, robbery, and aggravated assault, the NCVS includes sexual assault.
[c]The NCVS estimate includes sexual assault. See *Methodology* for details on the measurement of rape or sexual assault in the NCVS. The UCR estimate is based on the revised definition of rape.

Source: Bureau of Justice Statistics, National Crime Victimization Survey (NCVS), 2016; and FBI, *Crime in the United States*, 2016, https://ucr.fbi.gov/crime-in-the-u.s./2016/crime-in-the-u.s.-2016/topic-pages/tables/table-1.

Criminal Populations

In addition to police and victims, one common source for information on crime has been those serving "time" in the criminal justice system in either institutional or community corrections. Although recent years have revealed a downward decline in incarceration rates overall, the United States still far exceeds any other nation and its rate has quadrupled since the early 1970s. Examining this population reveals a lot about the systems priorities in terms of spending and practices. With an $80 billion price tag and annual cost per inmate ranging from $30,000 to $60,000, the financial and social cost of mass incarceration should hopefully not outweigh the benefits. Is this the case? There is no clear answer, however, with more than 2.1 million individuals in state and federal prisons and jails, and another 4.5 million under criminal justice supervision in the community, this population is a necessary part of the theoretical conversation. Whether it be in terms of race, age, region, socio-economic, or gender differentiation and disparity, or the general impact that being part of the corrections component has on the individual and their families. In more recent years, evidence-based practices that have a theoretical and research-based foundation, surpassing conventional knowledge and assumptions, have helped improve the effectiveness of treatment and alternatives to incarceration. But there is still a long way to go as recidivism rates hold at about 70%. It should become obvious why courses in corrections are a key component to any criminal justice degree program. In addition to appreciating the recent data highlighted below, see the Appendix for additional websites and resources.

The following are the highlights from a recent report on data regarding the correctional population in the United States:

- The incarcerated population in 2016 (2,162,400) fell to the lowest levels since 2004 (2,136,600).
- At the year-end of 2016, correctional officers supervised 6,613,500 offenders, which is a decrease of 0.9% during the year.
- 2016 marks the ninth consecutive year that the number of persons supervised by U.S. adult correctional systems has decreased.
- About 2.6% of adults in the United States (or 1 in every 38) were under some form of correctional supervision at the year-end of 2016, the lowest since 1993.
- At the year-end of 2016, the community supervision population was down 1.1% compared with the start of 2016, and the incarcerated population was down 0.5%. Both decreases are smaller than the percentage decrease seen between 2014 and 2015.
- In 2016, the major cause of the decline in the correctional population (80% of the decrease) was the drop in the community supervision population (down 49,800). This is greater than the decrease seen in 2015, with the major cause of that year's drop being the decrease in the prison population.
- By the year-end of 2016, the community supervision population (4,537,100) fell to the lowest level since 1999 (4,485,300).
- The decrease in the community supervision population during 2016 was due to a drop in the probation population (down 52,000).
- The incarcerated population decreased by 10,400 from 2015 to of 2016.

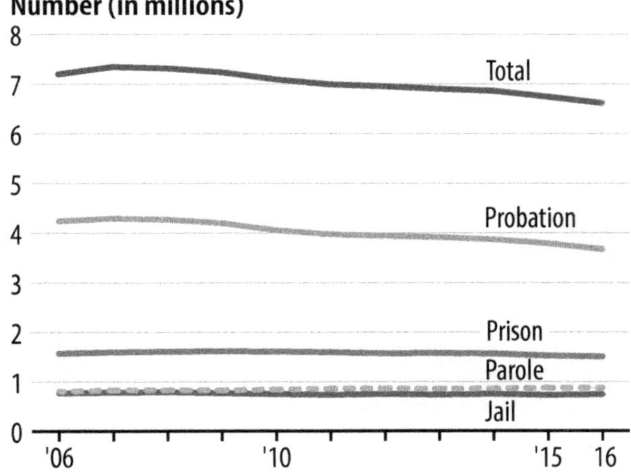

Figure 1.5 Total population under the supervision of U.S. adult correctional systems, 2006–2016.

Figure Credits

Fig. 1.1: Adapted from "The Challenge of Crime in a Free Society," A Report by the President's Commission on Law Enforcement and Administration Justice. 1967.

Table 1.1: Source: https://ucr.fbi.gov/nibrs/2016/tables/data-tables.

Table 1.2: Source: https://ucr.fbi.gov/nibrs/2016/tables/data-tables.

Table 1.3: Source: https://www.bjs.gov/content/pub/pdf/cv16.pdf.

Fig. 1.5: Source: https://www.bjs.gov/content/pub/pdf/cpus16.pdf.

Chapter 2

Organizing Theories

Like many things that are to be taught and learned, it is necessary to organize concepts and theories into groups. Many students find it a bit frustrating to not only have to commit to memory a certain theory, theorist, and key elements, but also to have to remember which broad category they belong to. However, it is essential to recognize that this field has come at the questions posed regarding criminals, their actions, thoughts, and contributing factors, through different lenses. Some of these approaches complement each other and some stand in opposition. Unlike mathematic equations, human behavior, the society we live in, our history, our laws, and our technology are evolving and changing. These changes will advance particular theories. Some theories will resurface and be added upon, while others may be buried for a while, if not forever. Some theories are continuing to evolve. In fact, many of the most fascinating and insightful theories in the field currently are ones that were not formulated until the 1990s. Even as I am writing this book, criminologists, sociologists, policy makers, and others are working on new concepts and theories.

In the application of theory, there is never going to be a perfect single match that will fully answer all questions relating to a certain criminal, criminal behavior, or policy trends, (i.e. punishment practices). The more options to choose from, the greater the chance for understanding.

Social and Political Context

One tool that will help students grasp the theoretical categories and appreciate their histories is understanding how policy and research are influenced by social and political context and ideologies. Social context asks the question, "What is going on in our society that might have an influence on how we view crime issues?" Political context asks the question, "How does the political ideology (the spectrum range from liberal to conservative) of our society and/or the individuals who are formulating law and policy shape the direction of policy and research and inquiry?" An example that can be used to display both concepts at work might be the legal and political changes that have taken place in our society since the 9/11 terror attacks.

Other reflections of this can be seen by analyzing the history and current controversies surrounding policies on immigration, gun control, distracted driving laws, and the original creation and recent considerations to resurrect three strikes laws.

Political Ideology

The dynamic of how social context and political ideology relate to the study of crime theory is fluid. It changes from location to location and behavior to behavior. A simple way to make the distinction between the two main opposing ideologies, conservative and liberal, is to consider how each views the root causes of crimes. The conservative sees the source within the individual criminal and believes that punishment should be at the individual level. With the extreme conservative, there is little to no regard for the underlying reasons for the individual's poor moral development. After all, the issues of poverty, family dysfunction, and racism, for example, are evident in the lives of many, yet not all turn to crime. The liberal ideology, while not excusing crime, recognizes that the ultimate criminal is a society that generates larger social forces subjecting its members to living life on the edge. This phenomenon is commonly referred to as *social marginality*. To the liberal, finding the answer to the crime problem requires analyzing social marginality. Research and policy stemming from this ideology may focus on the institutions of school, family, and the economy to address the overall crime problem. Research and policy stemming from a more conservative view will lean more toward proving the effectiveness of harsh punishment to stop criminals.

Categories of Theory

Over the years I have found that it is best for students to understand the major differences between the broad theoretical categories before launching into the individual theories. While there are several ways that traditional academic texts divide theories on crime and deviance, I have chosen the following format simply because it reflects a general consensus that many authors choose, and the distinctions are relatively easy to comprehend. The remainder of this chapter aims to identify the categories and briefly explain what makes each unique. Chapters three through seven will then take each category and elaborate on selected theories. Chapter eight will introduce students to recent concepts and models surrounding the very pressing issue of how drugs and crime are related. Not every theory will be mentioned or reviewed in detail. It is part of my pedagogical philosophy that it is best for students to develop a deep understanding of a few, often contrasting theories, as opposed to have a vague understanding of a more comprehensive list of many theories.

Five Main Broad Theoretical Categories

- Neo-classical theories
- Structure theories
- Process theories
- Conflict theories
- Developmental theories

Neo-Classical Theories

Have you ever watched a news story or observed a friend, family member, or acquaintance engaging in criminal behavior and asked yourself, "What were they thinking?" It is a very reasonable question to ask, but within the question lies an assumption that humans think before they act. Neo-classical theories are a group of theories that address the assumption that criminals are calculated thinkers. The roots of these theories developed out of *Deterrence theory* (commonly referred to as a philosophy of punishment). Deterrence is a school of thought that states that a criminal will resist behavior that will bring about negative costs (i.e. incarceration). However, if the criminal believes that the cost is not imminent, and/or the benefits of their activity outweigh the costs, then they will choose crime or deviance. Note the word "choose." Choice implies that we think before we act. In other words, criminals choose crime once they have spent time contemplating their behavior.

If we were to apply the basic premise of neo-classical theory to a practically universal adult experience, it would look something like this:

No one drives the speed limit because no one really wants to drive, say, 30 mph on a back road on the way to school. Why? Possible answer: going at least five to ten miles over the speed limit provides a benefit of getting where you are going faster, and the threat of getting a ticket is relatively low.

But what if one day you saw a speed trap? Would you reconsider speeding the next day? According to the basic premise of neo-classical theory, of course you would. One would be a fool to continue doing something when one knows that the chances of being caught are high.

But what if you had several friends who had been stopped by that same speed trap who only received warnings. Would this influence your decision? What if you had just won the lottery and had all the money in the world to pay for speeding tickets. Would that change your mind? What if you had just gotten your license back after losing it for DUI and you were aware that one more ticket might cost you your license again? Would that change your mind? What if the car you were driving was not yours, but rather the only car that you and your family share? Would that change your mind?

The point is to get you thinking about exactly what it is people might think about, and to accept that the equation for calculating is not the same from person to person, or even within the same person, depending on his or her circumstances.

Despite the critique of theories that rely heavily on the notion of the criminal as a calculated thinker, these neo-classical theories are used in understanding certain criminal behaviors. They also have an appeal among law enforcement and those who work on crime prevention. The implication is that if you can figure out the equation (i.e. the thinking of a criminal), this encourages implementation of specific policies and tactics that intercede in the equation by introducing variables that might have an impact on the calculation and prevent certain crimes.

Neo-classical theories make a good case for the need to continue developing alternative perspectives, as there are many criminal behaviors that cannot be adequately addressed by this category. Many criminals, when posed with the question, "What were you thinking?" might respond with "What are you talking about?" because they don't remember. Also, in more expressive crimes that are driven by intense emotions such as rage or jealousy, the calculated moments are often very brief and motivated by instant gratification, with little to no reflection on the cost. Other theoretical principles help address these examples that fall outside the realms of deterrence and neo-classical theories.

Structure Theories

According to structure theories, the answer for part one of Sutherland's definition of Criminology, "Why do people break the law?" is derived from the structure of society and the major social forces of social class, location, and the influence of subcultural and societal values and norms. Structure theories represent the first modern-day category of theories that came out of the Chicago school. Chicago is the birthplace of sociology, and during the turn of the twentieth century, with the Industrial Revolution well underway, cities like Chicago faced a myriad of social problems. Many of these social problems were directly and indirectly related to crime. Poverty, drug use, alcohol use, organized crime, overcrowding, illness, etc. crippled citizens. With the steady rise of the academic field of sociology, well-known scholars, many of whom came to the city of Chicago from the countryside to study crime, emerged.

It is important to appreciate that the social context at this time dictated that crime was basically a lower class, inner city phenomenon. In other words, to study crime all one had to do was study poor, inner city, delinquent boys to gain insight and in turn solve the crime problem. While some view structure theories as biased and ethnocentric, they do provide insight into inner city crime and may be used today to understand crime among the lower and working classes, as well as the influence of neighborhood and subculture regardless of location.

Process Theories

If you find the idea that the crime problem essentially lies among our poor, inner city, and underprivileged individuals in society offensive, you are not alone. To suggest that your social class or your neighborhood are the only predictors of criminal behavior is not just ethnocentric, it is factually unsound. As college students, many of you are part of middle and upper middle-class structures in society and were raised in suburbs and small-town communities. And guess what, this part of our society commits crime too! During the time that structure theories were being developed in Chicago, not all scholars of the early 1900s were content to rely on these theories as the end all be all to understanding crime. So, to these scholars, consideration must be given to how the explanation for crime is found foremost within the individual as opposed to in societal structure. In other words, understanding why poor people commit crime is a valid question, but the question of why any individuals commit crime regardless of social class, neighborhood, gender, age, etc. is also worthy of consideration.

Process theories help fill in the gap that structure theories do not adequately address. This category of theory can be used to develop intervention and policies on a micro level. Most students will find that they are able to relate better to process theories in understanding their own direct and indirect experiences with deviance and/or crime.

Conflict Theories

Conflict theory gained popularity during the 1970s, and today is a central part of understanding not only why people commit crime, but the connection between law making and reacting to law breakers. This category of theory takes a different approach. It is more concerned with why and how certain behaviors are defined as "criminal" in the first place. Conflict theories are not intimidated about questioning the status quo and asking the uncomfortable questions that suggest bias and discrimination exist in today's criminal justice system. This category also acknowledges that there is inequality, both intended and unintended, which produces laws that target certain minority groups in our society. Further, this category of theory acknowledges that power is distributed unequally, and that the main sources of power—social class, gender, race, and ethnicity—are used in our society to define and punish groups of people accordingly. While this theoretical category does focus more on the demise of the powerless, it also raises awareness of how recognition of conflict is a necessary agent for social change and ensuring equal protection under the law. This outcome is evidenced by the ongoing reviews of police practices such as racial profiling or how rape victims are treated. Because this category of theories has gotten a lot of recent attention in research and academia, a limited overview will be provided in this text. However, many students pursuing a degree program in criminal justice will have the opportunity to take, and will in many cases be required to take, entire courses that focus on the premises of conflict theory.

Developmental Theories

During the mid-1980s and into the 1990s, our society was fast approaching a peak of violent crime.

Much of this crime is committed by repeat offenders, many of whom were under community correctional supervision. The now-famed "three strikes law" came out of the social contextual cry of "We need to do something!" There were highly publicized tragedies of brutal killings by repeat offenders. Society at large recognized the need to get tough on crime given the wave of violence and drugs plaguing the nation. This spurred researchers, theorists, and policy makers to consider a new focus. And given the fact that a majority of serious crimes in our society are committed by a small, yet consistent population of criminals, it made sense to review cohort and longitudinal research established by earlier criminologists as well as to launch new research. The goal was to reach some conclusion about how a career criminal develops and stays committed to their criminal lifestyle. More importantly, this level of inquiry may impact crime reduction by discovering effective ways to stop these types of criminals in their paths before it is too late. The goal is also to be sure that when we say "this person is a lost cause," we are fairly certain before committing to the financial and social costs of lengthy incarceration.

This category of theory proposes that career criminals develop and are influenced by many of the factors set forth by structure and process theories. However, exactly how these factors play a role in the development of a career criminal receives special attention. What is encouraging about developmental theory is that if a recipe for crime can be discovered, and various red flags for failure and green flags for success can be identified with a fair degree of accuracy, our policies, practices, and resources can be put to better use.

While many of the theories have practical implications, developmental theory is especially attractive to students who will be working with offenders, or even young people in school or community settings who are at risk of developing lives of crime; developmental theory can reveal critical events that mold both the negative and positive turns lives can take.

Drug Concepts and Models

It is common sense that drugs are related to criminal activity. Whether it is the prostitute supporting a drug habit, or a sixteen-year-old boy exposed to drugs through his peers, the relationship is clear. The "which comes first, the chicken or the egg" analogy goes both ways and reveals the complexity of how drugs and crime are related. Currently, social and political context indicates that society is more accepting of marijuana use than ever, as evidenced by the decriminalization and legalization movements. For some, this type of action might indicate that drugs are not as troublesome as once thought. Let it not be said. With the resurgence of methamphetamine and its various forms (i.e. "ice"), prescription painkiller abuse, street heroin use, binge drinking among young adults, and the violence surrounding the importation and trafficking of many drugs (including marijuana), it is empirical how illegal drugs impact our society. In addition to violent crime that is connected to illegal drug activity, many states are also encountering rates of overdoses of prescription drugs, heroin, and cocaine that surpass the rates of the number of people killed in automobile accidents. And while students of criminal justice and/or related programs should no doubt take a course that focuses directly on drugs in our society, any theory course would be remiss not to bring awareness to some of the specific observations as to how drugs and crime are related. By the time students get to this subject matter, they will have achieved more insight as to why anyone may first use or continue to use and abuse drugs and/or alcohol. This may be explained through the variety of theories discussed to date. However, Paul Goldstein's (1985) models on how drug use sponsors crime have been found to isolate certain crime typologies and scenarios to help all professionals within the administration of justice better understand and intervene, with crime reduction as the goal.

Chapter 3

Neo-Classical Theories

What were you thinking? How does the thinking pattern of a criminal impact their behavior?

Deterrence Theory

Deterrence is a well-known philosophy of punishment associated often with the "crime doesn't pay" warning. While deterrence philosophy dates to the eighteenth century, it was revived during the 1970s in the United States as the social and political context called for a return to incarceration and stern punishment in response to the various upheavals of this time period. The main premise of deterrence theory is that criminals *choose* crime and that the choice of crime triumphs when the benefit of the crime outweighs the cost. In other words, criminals are free-will thinkers who contemplate their behavior and choose crime when it does pay. This theory works well with anyone looking to use punishment as the way to reduce crime by manipulating the "costs" so that they will outweigh the benefits of crime (i.e. make the cost high enough and the criminal will then be deterred from criminal behavior). Additionally, deterrence theory asserts that an increase in punishment can both specifically deter the individual offender and generally deter others in society who are contemplating starting or continuing in their criminal ways. These are more commonly referred to as ***general*** and ***specific*** deterrence. This theory is simplistic and easy to relay, but it has major flaws. However, society continues to evaluate the flaws in reconsidering existing policies. To appreciate the criticism, it is important to understand three additional elements associated with deterrence theory:

- **Severity** (how harsh or how lenient is the punishment?)
- **Celerity** (also called Swiftness) (how much time lapses between the crime and the punishment?)
- **Certainty** (do criminals really think they are going to be caught?)

Imagine being a parent who gets a call from their child's middle school reporting that their son/daughter swore at a teacher and that they felt that you as the parent should know and would be the best suited to respond to the situation—putting you in charge of the punishment. When your "tweenager" returns home at the end of the day, would you say, "I just got a call from the school. I am not sure if I am going to address this behavior, but if I do, I'd like to speak with you about it in a year. And if I decide to punish you I will be taking your video game privilege away for five minutes." Sounds crazy! It is. Would this deter the child's cursing issue in the future? Of course not. Yet, this is how punishment is often dealt with in the realities of the criminal justice system. Most criminals do not think they will be caught—because most aren't. The typical length of time between offense and punishment is often up to a year, if not more. Especially for first time petty and misdemeanor offenders, the punishments are not very harsh. And even in those cases when punishment is too harsh (as opposed to too lenient), this can create problems. If you were ever over-punished as a child, you can relate to the emotional and perhaps the negative behaviors that followed.

Of all three elements, the **perception of certainty** is the one that impacts criminals the most. If criminals perceive that they will or will not get caught, it may impact their choices. The American justice system requires that punishment not be too swift, and the wheels of justice turning slowly is something that we have come to accept and admire within our justice system. And while for certain types of crime, especially the most heinous, it may be difficult, especially for victims, to wait out this process, it is part of a due process system. When it comes to severity, it has been well established that criminals focus more on the benefits of their crime than the costs. Many are not even aware of the statutory minimums and maximums for their crimes.

Rational Choice Theory

Rational choice theory adds some considerations that provide more insight into the criminal as a rational thinking person. The two essential components are that there are multiple costs and rewards to be considered and that costs and benefits can be both ***tangible*** (such as property, money, incarceration) and ***intangible*** (such as emotions, fitting in with peers, thrill, etc.)

This theory is a good one to apply to crimes that often are misunderstood by the public. It is a decent theory to help devise policy and tactics to work with criminals who may need to readjust their thinking by facing underlying cost/benefit issues.

For example, someone who is stealing or dealing drugs to support a severe drug addiction has a different rational choice process than a teen who joins in on a violent bullying incident to avoid being teased by their peers. We all choose a variety of behaviors each day. Why suppose criminals are different?

The two main criticisms of this theory are that we do not know the degree to which criminals ponder, and that certain crimes fit this theory better than others.

Routine Activities Theory

Routine activities theory is a theory that is well suited for crime prevention policies and law enforcement tactics. The common mistake students make with this theory is assuming that it focuses on the habits formed by criminals that make crime a routine. However, what this theory is really discussing is how the routines of victims and non-criminals impact the decisions and choices for criminals. This theory suggests that when there are changes in the routines of how members of society spend their time, they impact the selections of crime for the offenders.

There are three elements that this theory draws attention to for understanding how crime evolves.

- **Motivated Offender**—refers to the desire to offend, which can relate back to the intangible/tangible benefits and rewards.
- **Vulnerable Victims/Targets**—refers to the person or persons who will be the victims of the crime, whether it be a person, a store, or someone willing to purchase drugs, etc.
- **Lack of Capable and Suitable Guardians**—refers to people, surveillance cameras, and warning signs that may not exist, or if they do, their existence is not capable of, or suitable for, deterring crime. (NOTE: A parent who is home is only suitable for preventing what delinquency is going on in the home to the extent they are paying attention.)

Over the years, the following true case scenario has also helped students appreciate this theory. Below is the scenario. Read the following and then contemplate how each of the elements can be seen at play:

> Two young men were able to print counterfeit US currency using access they had to their parents' high-tech computer in a home office that was often left unattended. Even when the parents were home, they were not attentive to what materials had been used in the office. Upon obtaining the online recipe for printing the currency, these individuals realized they could not simply go on a shopping spree for fear of getting caught with hundreds of counterfeit bills. So instead, they devised a scheme where they would go through various drive-thru fast food restaurants during times of the day that were not crowded. They would then order a single cheap item, preferably from a dollar-type menu, pay with a fake bill, and get authentic currency for change. After going through dozens of drive-thru, they were then able to take their legitimate bills and venture a few towns away to a large shopping outlet for a shopping spree.

Activity: Discuss how Routine Activities Theory might explain the above case study. Consider the following questions in your analysis.

What about these young men might have motivated them?
What about society and the way we buy fast food makes this crime possible?
What about the time of day reduced the risk of getting caught?

One of the consistent critiques of using this theory in practice and policy stems from a concept called *crime displacement*. In sum, crime displacement recognizes that some criminals will change the type of crime, the location, or even the method once they see that law enforcement has caught on to them. The trouble then arises when a community may think they have solved a crime in their community, when in reality, it may have moved to another community or underground. For example, when I was working at a federal probation office in Burlington, VT, I was surprised by the number of urban drug organizations that had set up camp in Burlington that were not "home grown." While most of the drug dealers were locals, there were a disproportionate number of dealers who had left the larger inner cities of Massachusetts, Connecticut, and New York because of crackdowns and tough enforcement in their communities during the war on drugs. Under this scenario, then, how effective were those strategies, really?

Summary

Neo-classical theories all suggest that criminals think before they act. Their decisions are impacted by factors such as perceived punishment, whether the punishment is worth the benefit, and societal and circumstantial changes that cause criminals to select certain crimes and certain times. While these theories do not fully explain crime, they do help students understand how to theoretically explain criminal behavior in a fairly straightforward manner.

Activity: To test your own analytical abilities, attempt to explain some of the following behaviors using any of the neo-classical theories. When done, return to your explanation and suggest a way to catch, reduce, or prevent the behavior according to your analysis:

- Drunk driving
- Sexual assaults on dormed college campuses
- Underage drinking
- Smoking cigarettes
- Cheating on an exam
- Burglary

Chapter 4

Structure Theories

How do the physical structure of where you live, the value structure of your society, and the values and norms and thinking patterns of the subculture you are a part of influence what you think about and what you do?

In this chapter, **three sub-categories** of structure theory will be discussed: **ecological theories, anomie/strain theories, and subculture theories.**

Ecology Theories

Where You Live

Social Disorganization Theory

During the turn of the twentieth century, with the Industrial Revolution well underway, the rapid growth of cities due to migration to cities in the north brought the issues commonly associated today with city life—poverty, crime, and substance abuse—to the surface. The city of Chicago became an especially attractive place to study given its size, its layout, and it also being the birthplace of sociology. The University of Chicago remains one of the leaders in this academic field, which has dominated much of crime theory. Commonly referred to as the Chicago School, the early inquiries and theories are among some of the first to academically approach the study of criminal behavior.

Social disorganization theory was developed by Clifford R. Shaw and Henry D. McKay (1969) and utilized the works of other theorists whose main focus was on the relationship between living in the city and negative behavior. This theory followed along with the ideas set forth by concentric zone theory (Ronald Park and Ernest Burgess), which illustrated how certain cities that are laid out with a center and radiation outward (like a bull's-eye) seem to attract the most crime in the transition zone just outside the center. While many cities, such as Boston, are not mapped out this way, Chicago is a city that has this design, and studying how where you live impacts your access to criminal opportunity remains an area of study today even for cities that do not mirror the layout of Chicago. All cities, and for that matter large and small towns, have areas where crime rates are consistently higher than other parts of the city or town, regardless of the demographic changes within that specific area.

Social disorganization theory draws on the assumption that all of us, regardless of where we live, rely on the social ties in our community and the strength of the closeness of our relationships with family and neighbors to help control and, in many cases, watch over each other's behavior. Shaw and McKay observed that people living in densely populated and impoverished areas where there is a lot a hustle and bustle and many new faces (such as was the case in Chicago due to migration and immigration) will find it harder to govern and control the lives of those around them and, in turn, will pass down their chaotic and delinquent behaviors and values to the next generation, thus resulting in a cycle of delinquency. Social disorganization refers to the weakened social ties that exist in the cities and especially in certain parts of cities. Based on the early premise within the social sciences that one of the strongest aspects to a healthy society is the ability that its members must control, encourage, and care for its members, social disorganization theory was able to support this by pointing out higher crime rates in the city. Given that this theory was developed during the early 1900s and came out of the first groups of theories within modern crime theory, it remains open to criticism. Even today, many are hesitant to suggest that the root of all criminal behavior can be explained simply in where one lives. However, it is a good place to start. And the fact that it brings about ethnocentric concerns helped fuel other theorists both at that time period and today. The bottom line is that there are many who live in the city and even come from generations of city dwellers from the worst side of town who do not engage in delinquent activity. What is the difference? While there is no clear answer, the fact that the question remains supports the need to further explore criminal theories, many of which will be introduced in the pages of this text.

Dangerous Deviant Places Theory

In the same vein as social disorganization theory, Rodney Stark (1987) developed a theory that also focuses on how one's residence affects behavior and crime rates in certain neighborhoods. Therefore, it is considered an ecological theory. This theory combines the premises of social disorganization theory with routine activities theory by showing how location can also create more motivated offenders and opportunities for crime due to the lack of guardians and social control in certain areas. Today, law enforcement personnel recognize that there are certain "hot spots" for crime and even certain types of crimes in cities across our country. Even smaller city and town police officers and residents will acknowledge that there are those parts of the community known for higher rates of criminal behaviors. To help provide more insight into this phenomenon, Stark highlighted some additional factors and variables that help explain why higher rates of crime are present in certain neighborhoods. A summary of these factors and variables is provided below.

- **Transience:** People moving in and out of an area at high rates.
- **Density:** A lot of people living in a small amount of space.

- **High degree of rental units:** People are less invested in property they do not own.
- **Urban decay:** Unkept space such as parks, playgrounds, and abandoned homes and cars, and trash is more apparent in these areas.
- **Mixed use areas:** Living close by to places where people are doing more than living, such as shopping, buying lottery tickets, visiting restaurants, bars, and plazas, loitering, etc.
- **Increased contact with strangers:** Due to transience, density, and demographic shifts in the population.
- **Cynical residents and cynical law enforcement:** A negative and poor, "I give up" outlook and attitude that develops among some residents and law enforcement.
- **Reduction in social control creating more opportunity for crime:** All the above factors make certain areas easier to access for criminal activity.

The above factors are fairly self-explanatory, especially if you have ever lived or gotten lost in a city with high crime. Further analysis of the above factors will be reviewed in class as necessary.

Summary

The suggestion that living in the city places you at higher risk for being an offender and/or victim of crime is nothing startling. But these ideas and the theories developed from them do hold a place in understanding criminal behavior. Looking at cities remains a key focus for those involved in policies aimed at reducing crime. However, these theories have their limits. The main criticism is that these theories are accusatory and can come across as offensive to many of our law-abiding citizens from the city. We should also be mindful that not everyone has the luxury of deciding where they want to live. Also, studies have shown that life in the ghettos and urban enclaves of our country are not as "disorganized" as assumed. There are also many inner-city neighborhoods in which there is a great sense of pride despite lack of property ownership, and this should be honored and recognized.

Anomie Theories

How societal values and outside social forces add stress and strain to your life and influence your behavior.

Anomie Strain Theory

This theory is one of the most well-known and is a good place to start in understanding how a society's values influence criminal and other deviant behavior. Robert Merton (1968) put forth the idea that living in a society that places a high level of importance on materialistic financial success as a core value places stress and strain on its members. However, for most of us, we resolve this by taking advantage of the wide array of socially approved methods (commonly referred to as means) to achieve such success. There is not just one legitimate road to success. Options range from getting a good job to learning a trade, going to college, marrying someone who can financially support you, etc. The key is that none of these options are criminal.

Per this theory, the above resolution to the goals vs. means struggle is referred to by Merton as *conformity*. But this is just one of five different ways to approach the strain upon us all from living in our society. The four additional approaches help elaborate on other resolutions. These resolutions are sometimes referred to as *modes of adaptation*. Below are the additional four modes with brief explanations. In-class examples and documentary case studies will help further analyze:

Innovator: A person who accepts the goal of success but rejects the institutionalized means. Example: Someone who wants a car but can't afford one might steal one or use money derived from other criminal proceeds to get a car.

Ritualist: A person who has given up on success but, due to their ethics and moral standing, will not reject the means and therefore will not resort to crime. Example: A tired single mother living in a housing project with little to no financial support from her estranged husband, who will continue to work, maybe even several jobs, to keep food on the table, even though she has given up on the idea that her hard work will bring her material success. While she is not a criminal, her behavior attitude is not desirable and may impact her children and her community at large as seen in some of the other structure theories previously discussed.

Retreatist: A person who has given up on success, but is not willing to go through the motions like a ritualist. The retreatist will fill their time using and possibly abusing drugs, adopting a lazy, poor work ethic, and/or struggling to maintain healthy intimate relationships. Example: A thirty-year-old who is still living at home in their parent's basement working a menial job that pays enough to buy a bag of weed and a thirty pack on the weekends. Retreatists are criminal in the sense that they may be using illicit drugs or scamming the welfare or unemployment system, but they are not the more serious offenders like the innovators. Nonetheless, retreatists drain our society and their families, and efforts to reduce retreatist mentality are worthy, yet often not a top priority of the criminal justice system. If people have no goals and have given up on success, then their lifestyles will not be all that impressive. I once heard someone say, "If you aim hard enough at nothing, you will get it." This is a retreatist mentality.

Rebel: A person who does not buy into the social values of success and recreates their own meaning of success, therefore requiring their own means that will help them achieve their new goals. Example: Hate criminals and terrorists are not interested in material success. They are motivated by hatred or political or religious agenda, making this type of criminal more complex to understand and predict.

This theory has its limits, but it was never intended to fully explain criminal behavior. It does help us understand how essential it is to appreciate that not all criminals are motivated by the same forces.

General Strain Theory

Robert Agnew's (2001) general strain theory takes the assumptions of anomie strain theory and adds a psychological component so that we can better understand additional structural forces that can come upon an individual that might lead them to harbor emotions associated with criminal and delinquent behavior. This theory is attractive to advocates who see psychological stressors working along with social structural forces.

The sources of strain are identified for this theory:

1. *Failure to achieve goals*
Examples: Not just the goal of financial success, but failing grades, a failed sports goal, a failed relationship, marriage, etc.

2. *Removal of positive stimuli: people, relationships, and things that we cherish*
Examples: Death, illness, moving, a bad break up, or even the threat of any of these.

3. *Presence of noxious stimuli: negative events, people, and social forces*
Examples: Abuse, financial burden, natural disasters, or even the threat of any of these.

Agnew asserts that any or all of these sources produce feelings of frustration and low self-esteem, which are powerful emotions that can lead to self-destructive and socially destructive behaviors.

But we all know better than to think that some people are free of these sources of strain. The reality is we all have these elements, and some of us have quite a bit more than others. The real question here is what is it that makes some people able to face and overcome stressors without turning to crime while others cannot manage without turning to crime. According to this theory, the magic words are *coping skills*. The ability to cope with life's struggles is a skill that is developed over time through a combination of the forces of socialization and individual temperament. Those who can cope are better insulated from crime. In order to address crime in our society, it may make sense to not only address sources of strain, but to work better on developing coping skills so that when these structural forces come along we are better able to manage the associated emotive responses that may lead to destructive and criminal behavior.

One tip that I have found works well in developing coping skills, which I have used in counseling criminals and others struggling with destructive deviance, is to lower the expectations for those around you. This is not to suggest that if your spouse is cheating on you, or if one of your colleagues is sexually harassing you, that you should tolerate this type of behavior. However, if you go into the world expecting everyone to live up to a high standard and to never encounter struggles and imperfection, then it will be that much harder and frustrating for you when situations arise that produce stress and strain. I have seen students fall away from college because of one bad experience with a teacher who did not fit their ideal of what they expect from a professor. Life is not perfect. People are not perfect. Our institutions will forever be flawed. While more could be said about coping skills, the point here is to introduce this idea within the context of general strain theory to exemplify how a theory such as this can have real life strategy implications in the criminal justice setting.

Institutional Anomie

This final anomie theory is the most recent and draws upon Messner's and Rosenfeld's (2007) notion that by virtue of living in the United States you are part of a society that stresses the "American dream." This dream emphasizes not only material success, but individualism and achievement. The likelihood of this dream coming true, however, depends on the extent that our major institutions such as family, education, religion, economy, and politics are able to support its members as they embark on their journeys in pursuit of the dream. Unfortunately, and especially in more recent years, these institutions have shifted and evolved in a way that does not support many American dream chasers. For example, college tuitions, on average, are four times what they were thirty years ago. In other words, when the institutions start to crumble, and the stressors of life increase, for many the answer is to resort to crime to fulfill the dream.

While this theory is continuing to evolve, it is worthy of consideration. I would encourage students to look at outside sources that show the changing dynamics among various institutions. And while it is a broad-based macro theory, one of the important considerations it proposes is that perhaps we need to redefine what we mean by the American dream. If the dream changes, then the impacts of certain failing institutions may be less detrimental. By looking at this theory in combination with Merton's theory, and the emotional impact of Agnew's stressors, it is reasonable to look at how one of the many applications of this theory may lie in the social construction of the American dream.

Subculture Theories

How does being part of the subculture of our inner city lower classes provide a structure conducive to crime?

Status Frustration Theory

Status frustration (also referred to as reaction-formation theory), developed by Al Cohen (1955), illustrates well how belonging to one group or subculture and not another can impact behavior. In this case, it is being part of the lower class that exposes one to a subculture at heightened risk for crime and delinquency. This theory was introduced to provide explanations for primarily delinquent inner-city youth male crime. Once understood, however, this theory can be used to understand crime not only among lower class kids (hereafter referred to as LCKs) but also among working class kids in our cities and towns. This observation gives this theory modern-day appeal even though it was developed during the 1950s.

The sociological use of the term *status* refers to one's position in society. And the position being identified here is being poor and/or from the lower class. However, regardless of what social stratum you find yourself in, you live in a society that is based on middle class values. These values are portrayed in mass media, in education systems, and within social interactions in various social settings. And being below or "less" than the majority does not produce good emotions. On the contrary, it produces a sense of frustration and a feeling that life is not fair. It may cause a sense of resentment and anger toward the middle class and what they represent. This value system is often referred to as the "middle class measuring rod," consisting of values such as patience, sensitivity, delayed gratification, controlled emotion and aggression, making wise decisions when it comes to friendship, and understanding that it is not always in your best interest to remain loyal to the end to a friend who is making poor decisions. In response to this frustration, LCKs ridicule and essentially give the middle finger to the middle class with a negative attitude, which then results in the creation of a new set of values among the subculture of LCKs. This set of values is conducive to criminal behavior. Below are three values seen among the LCKs that, when analyzed, reveal this trashing of middle class values. See if you can understand which middle-class values are being ridiculed.

Lower/Working Class Values:

- Immediate gratification
- Untamed aggression
- Loyalty

Middle class youth are raised to appreciate having to wait and earn what they want. They are provided with opportunities to legitimately handle their aggression, whether it be in the context of school sports or just tussling around with family and friends in a safe and relatively controlled environment. Perhaps one of the most insightful parts of this theory is how loyalty is valued among the LCKs. This a term that often has positive connotations. Wouldn't we all like to be regarded as loyal friends, parents, children, etc? But there may be times in our lives when being loyal to the wrong people can put us in danger or prevent someone from saying "no" to opportunities and criminal behaviors that arise.

One case scenario that illustrates this loyalty value well involves the true story of a young man who became involved with dealing ecstasy, despite coming from a well-off suburb of Boston. Because his family was made up of poor, first generation Italians who worked as semi-skilled laborers, he was aware of his status. He was also surrounded by peers in social classes well above his own. However, there were enough kids like him in his town that they bonded together and formed a subculture. And when asked to help a friend drive to an airport many states away to secure the drugs, the only answer available was yes. Not only did he satisfy the immediate gratification for money and items that he and his friends could not obtain through legitimate means, he also felt he did not have any choice but to help and be loyal to his friendship. This sense of loyalty also reared its head a few years after his conviction and release from serving two years in a federal prison, when he allowed one of his buddies to smoke marijuana in his apartment and had the paraphernalia confiscated by his probation officer during a home visit. What was interesting about this case was that the young man did not smoke marijuana, yet his sense of loyalty to his friend prevented him from avoiding involvement in the drug conspiracy and later from not asking him to leave and smoke marijuana somewhere else. Neo-classical theory may address this as a clear-cut example of costs versus benefits calculus. But status frustration theory adds to the analysis by analyzing how decisions are influenced heavily by subcultures. And in this case, the reward of being loyal outweighed the cost of being caught in criminal activity or for violating conditions of release. This value is one of the hardest values to reverse in the reality of the lives of many struggling youths who rely on the loyalty of their friends for emotional and physical protection and security.

Focal Concerns Theory

It is important to understand that poverty and crime are not always correlated. However, another subculture theory developed during the 50s was one that also made sense among the youth of past, present, and future. Walter Miller (1958) viewed crime as a lower-class issue due to the mindset of being young, poor, and, in most cases, male. While he did not address gender, race, and ethnicity directly, elements of this theory have been expanded by modern theorists.

Before reviewing the key elements of this theory, consider the following situation my son faces as a teenager:

When my son was a freshman in high school, he was on Facebook discussing how excited he was to go to a local amusement park on the upcoming weekend. During his conversation, one of his female schoolmates (I like to call them gal pals) saw his posts. Being a fan of amusement parks, and having a season pass that was almost due to expire, she asked if she could come along. My son was able to get permission from the organizers of the field trip for his friend to attend. So off they went and enjoyed a day at the park with dozens of other kids from around the community. Come Monday morning, my son declared that he was not feeling well enough to go to school. Come to find out he was in fact a little scared to go to school, because it had been rumored that the gal pal who went along on the field trip was still involved with a boyfriend who was not impressed that my son had "taken his girl" on a date. Even though it was not a date, the situation presented itself. Long story short, my son set off to school with the proper parenting advice. Fortunately, he used words to resolve the issue with the other young boy, as he was a nervous wreck by lunchtime with the rumors flying high. As it turned out, the situation had been blown out of proportion by some nosey teens and the boy accepted my son's apology and laughed it off. Point? This was the only time during my son's high school years that he had ever shown this much fear and concern about going to school.

This is different than the type of fear and anxiety a student might have due to an exam. According to Miller, LCKs are faced with this negative anticipation on a regular, if not daily, basis. The emotional work that goes on in the brain of an LCK in being aware and prepared for what any day may present creates a level of concern that is only experienced on rare occasions, if at all, by middle class teens. These concerns are called focal concerns. Below is a list of the six main focal concerns that, according to Miller, consume the minds of LCKs, along with behaviors that are associated with criminal and delinquent behavior.

- **Trouble**—meaning avoiding trouble from enemies, police, and teachers, because it is lurking around every corner.
- **Toughness**—meaning being prepared for the trouble that might come your way. A readiness that might require you to carry a dangerous weapon or to prove your toughness by getting into verbal and physical altercations, so others know you are not to be messed with.
- **Smartness**—meaning being aware that to survive you must be aware that others are out to con you, and you need to be alert and able to sniff and snuff out the con before it happens. Conversely, you need to be your own sort of con to those around you, especially if you are involved in criminal activity such as dealing drugs or pawning stolen goods.
- **Excitement**—meaning that boredom is not an option. Life must be a constant thrill. And if it isn't, then you have to create the excitement. This concern is especially helpful in explaining higher dropout rates among our poor. When this is combined with the lower-class value of immediate gratification, it is easy to see why impulsive decisions to do things for the sake of the thrill are made.
- **Autonomy**—meaning to be free from having to do what anybody tells you to do. Anybody! This helps us understand why poor kids have a tougher time dealing with adults, school administrators, and law enforcement when confronted.
- **Fate**—meaning being aware daily that life is out of your control. You look around you and see people in your subculture getting caught up in the system, succumbing to substance abuse, or in many cases being injured or even killed long before their time. If this is all that is around you, it deflates your sense of working hard and planning for the future. Once you are not pursuing a future that you think is in your hands, then what reason is there to not take risks? Imagine if you really felt that you only had a ten percent chance of living past thirty. Would it change your decision about what you might ingest or the risky behaviors you might engage in? And now add on top of that the lack of a middle-class upbringing and education that teaches you that life does not have to be this way—insight into a lot of nonsensical violence and other crimes, especially among our lower classes, is gained.

This theory, of course, does not explain all crime. The fact that it neglects crimes among the rich is purposeful. It is important to remember to judge a theory based on the scope of its explanation.

Additional Subculture Theories

Below are two additional subculture theories that expand upon the above ideas and provide some excellent insight and further consideration. For the sake of time, the highlighted additions are noted in summary fashion.

Differential Opportunity (Cloward and Ohlin, 1960)

Not all lower-class youth are exposed to the same opportunities to succeed. And not all are exposed to the same opportunities to commit crime. Depending on the area, the criminal climate of the time, abilities, skills, and restrictions, being part of the lower class does not produce one particular type of criminal. If a person is not connected to a drug ring, they may have to resort to another type of crime to occupy their time, due to a lack of criminal and non-criminal opportunities. Imagine being frustrated not only because you don't have the opportunities to succeed in the legitimate world, but you also have no open access to the money-making underground world of crime? This theory helps give insight into why some parts of the lower-class culture finds themselves in subcultures that are focused on violence, as opposed to making money, as opposed to burning out on drugs. It all depends on the different opportunities. This helps support investigating crime opportunity within and among different impoverished areas throughout our country to be sure that policies and interventions are aimed at the right targets and are addressing the most prevalent issues.

Code of the Street (Elijah Anderson, 1999)

The final subculture theory well worth mentioning is that which suggests that good and decent people can be found in inner cities and that sometimes, good people find themselves making poor decisions. Unlike neo-classical theory, this subculture theory attempts to expand on what influences the decisions and behaviors, specifically, in this theory, among inner city, poor African Americans. This theory can also be stretched to understand crime by other demographic groups. However, given the sharp rise in inner city homicide rates, violent crime, and gang activity in the mid-80s and 90s, Anderson's desire to compile through ethnographic research various elements of this subculture is well deserved. While there are challenges and legitimate critiques in approaching this line of theory, it does provide a level of insight that criminal justice practitioners, criminologists, and society must recognize. A central theme to the code of the street theory is that there are unwritten informal rules of conduct that govern people who live in certain types of environments. The rules are understood through informal communication, and it is passed down from one generation to the next that these rules exist and must be obeyed to survive. Imagine moving into a housing project as a single mother with two teenage African American boys. There would be obvious rules presented in the landlord–tenant agreement that you may or may not share with your sons. However, you would not see on this tangible list of rules an instruction that your sons must never engage in direct eye contact with another young person's girlfriend, or that they must try their best, even if it means through illegal activity, to have a new fresh-looking outfit on a daily basis and that being an outfit repeater would be considered a "sin." However, it is these latter rules about how to gain respect, avoid being disrespected, and avoid trouble that may be lifesaving. The central theme to the code is respect. Expect it, defend it, and if lost, regain it, and quick!! Anderson's work is expansive, and the elements of the code are plentiful and have made their way into the genre of understanding urban crime. This theory also is helpful in looking at socialization, parenting styles, and attitudes that come with living in a community of despair and hopelessness that once again gives sensitivity to understanding that thinking patterns may differ depending on the subculture.

Summary

Subculture theories offer a wealth of insight and knowledge, which at times can seem ethnocentric and stereotypical. However, they are accepted at large in the criminological community with the understanding that they must be viewed, analyzed, and applied in the proper context. It is important to remember that we are all humans and that no one can choose the situation they are born into. And given that much of this theoretical category focuses on teen and young adult violence, many of these individuals also cannot choose their residence during this time period in their lives. Subculture theories also address the areas of male versus female subculture, violent subculture, and the role of gender. For further inquiry, the following are three key, yet controversial, have developed out of this crime theory category:

- Marvin Wolfgang and Franco Ferracuti's (1982) subculture of violence theory
- Mead Chesney-Lind (1973), James Messerschmidt (1997), and others—feminist criminology
- John Hagen's (1989) power-control theory

Activity: Devise a list of questions that as a school principal, or chief of police, you would want to investigate to help control crime in your community that reflect an understanding of a subculture theory. Do your best to highlight key elements of the specific theory.

Chapter 5

Process Theories

The Company You Keep And How You Feel About Yourself

Don't underestimate the role of your self-concept, your distribution of time, the influence of others on your behavior, and how you feel and think about what you do! As noted in Chapter 2, process theories are more individualized and steer away from the somewhat restricted focus of structure theories. Although some process theories can easily be combined and related to structure theories as plausible explanations of crime, they do warrant separate consideration.

In this chapter, **three subcategories** of structure theory will be discussed: **association and drift theories, social control theories**, and **labeling theories.**

Association and Drift Theories

After a recent lecture about association and drift theories, a student raised her hand and said, "So basically, this is about what my mother used to say to me 'watch the company you keep!'" In many ways, this statement exemplifies the essence of the first theory that will be introduced in this chapter.

Differential Association

Theory

As set forth by Edwin Sutherland (1972), the key to this theory is that crime is learned behavior. But it is not just the "how to" skills involved in stealing a car or packaging and distributing drugs; there are attitudes that go along with these behaviors. According to Sutherland (1972), there is no such thing as a born criminal. There is also no guarantee that just because you are shown how to commit a crime that you will do so. There is also no reality in which young people and/or adults never encounter criminal elements. However, what is key about this theory is that the extent to which individuals fall into a criminal lifestyle depends on the nature of the face-to-face contact we have with those in our primary groups. There are many formal and informal social groups that we are connected to, especially during adolescence. Some of these groups are good for us and help us learn skills and attitudes that will carry us far in life.

Other groups, while they may seem appealing at the time, especially during our most rebellious years, teach us skills and attitudes that can be destructive and make us susceptible to criminal activity. Sutherland's theory in its raw form has nine propositions and four key elements. While I find these wordy concepts intriguing and insightful, I appreciate that for today's introductory student, the "lingo" Sutherland uses can be confusing. Therefore, I have simplified the essential components of his theory. First, it is key to understand that according to *differential association*, crime is learned through time spent with other deviants and criminals. Appreciating that time, by default, is also distributed is also key. In other words, it is impossible to be in two places at the same time. The elements of **frequency** and **duration** are also key to this theory, meaning that how much time spent between different groups and the duration of the time spent will impact how we are swayed by our associations' criminal habits and attitudes that are not favorable toward law-abiding behavior, whether it be skipping school, doing drugs, stealing, and so on. The elements of **priority** and **intensity** help us understand the degree of seriousness of the behavior, and whether or not we are casual observers, we give our minds over to the group so that it becomes a priority for us. In sum, crime can be explained on an individual level by looking at the details and day-to-day lives of the individual criminal, surroundings, peer group, distribution of time, and the amount of mental energy that is given to the different types of social interactions.

One way to think about this theory is how the line, "You can lead a horse to water but you can't make it drink" can be stretched into "You can lead a horse to water, and you might make it drink, but if it doesn't get led often, and can't stand the taste of water, and has better things to do with its time, it may not continue to drink water."

When I was in high school, we had much more freedom than high school students of today, such as having a smoking area and permission to leave campus during study blocks, and there was no such thing as a junior operating license. I can remember being a freshman in high school, hanging out in the smoking area (even though I didn't smoke), when a girl asked me if I wanted to go "cruisin'" during lunch block with some boys. It sounded fun, so we went to the parking lot, where we were met by two boys. I was not sure of their ages, but they were somewhere between sixteen and eighteen. My relatively new-found friend and I hopped in the back seat, and off we went. As we crossed into the next town, where the McDonald's was, we stopped for gas. It was a quick stop and a full-service station. Then, within a few minutes, we stopped for gas again. And then again. All at different full-service stations. At the third gas station, I realized that the driver was running a scam by asking for five dollars of gas and then insisting that he had paid with a twenty instead of a ten-dollar bill. He was intimidating, and given the time of day, the gas servers were older gentlemen who looked like they had seen better days and were not up to challenging the teen, so they dispensed the money. After the third stop, we proceeded to McDonald's and then went to one of the boys' apartments, where I observed drug paraphernalia and a discussion between the two about stashing some of the money they had scored from their scam. They laughed at how easy it was and that gas was overpriced anyway. We were dropped back off at school, and that was the last time I took my "friend" up on an offer to go hang with who she regarded as "cool" guys.

Activity: See if you can pull key elements from differential association theory to explain both the deviance and criminality of the two boys, as well as why I was not drawn into their crime world. In your analysis, consider what other pieces of information you would want to know to fully appreciate the differences between the boys, the girl, and myself.

Techniques of Neutralization

Drift Theory

Are criminals, criminals all the time? What do you think?

Consider the following scenario as this next theory is introduced. While working at an inner-city residential prerelease program that housed approximately fifty male offenders who had served time in a house of correction in Boston, just this line of questioning was presented by my then-four-year-old daughter. First, assume this brief background. The facility was a five-story brownstone in a residential neighborhood in Boston. There was no in-house security such as an armed guard, electronic locks, or panic buttons. While most residents were there for theft, drug dealing, alcohol-related assaults, and disorderly conduct, most of the residents met the profile of a typical inner-city street punk. My role was to assist in program development, and in the evenings, I would run life skills sessions with the residents. I had taken the job on a part-time basis so that I could work in the criminal justice system but be able to spend most of my days and nights as a "stay at home mom" with my newborn son and daughter. The pay was not that great, but I found the experience most rewarding for my growth in understanding of this particular criminal population. One particular evening when I returned from work my husband brought to my attention that my daughter had what he thought was a very important question: "Why does mommy have to work with those bad boys?" She went on to express fear and concern in the words of a toddler. My husband, however, translated the message just fine. But what they did not understand was that while these residents had done some "bad" things, they were not bad 100% of the time. And when it came to time spent in the program, they were rarely out of line or required disciplinary action. How could this be? Well, Sykes and Matza (1957) have developed a theory that addresses this very issue, which addresses the question, why are criminals not criminal all the time? Given the concern my family raised about the residents in the program, part of my discussion with my husband was to point out the following about the residents:

- They were not under the influence of drugs and alcohol while in the program.
- They would consider any personal assaults or financial crimes against me despicable, as they would be genuinely concerned about my well-being and were aware of how important my possessions were to me.
- I was a person in their eyes, someone they saw as a way out of their negative lifestyle who sincerely wanted to help them.

- They didn't find my approach corrupt or insensitive, nor did they think I was abusing my position.
- They desired to get their freedom and knew that abiding by the rules of society and the program was so important that other types of "codes" and rules they might answer to on the streets did not apply in the program.

Sykes and Matza (1957) assert that criminals use a set of rationalization excuses and justifications to convince themselves that their crime is not really a crime, or at the very least is okay. This mindset helps to neutralize the behavior from being criminal to being neither criminal nor noncriminal, or, in some cases, normal. These rationalizations are referred to as the *techniques of neutralization* and are noted below. Notice how each one can be used to explain why my family's concerns were understandable, yet not valid.

Five Techniques of Neutralization

1. **Denial of responsibility**—blaming behavior on outside influence such as drugs, alcohol, and outside pressures.
2. **Denial of injury**—rationalizing that no one is really getting hurt. This is common in property theft crimes and among drug dealers. In fact, at the residential program I worked for almost a year with a young serial car thief who, to his surprise, was angered at the idea that someone might steal my car while I was working late at night. He knew enough about my family to know that we had only one car, two small children, and were living paycheck to paycheck. But in his arrogance, he would separate himself from most of the other residents, whom he felt were real "scum bags" because they did drugs and hurt people. To him, his crimes didn't hurt anyone. Or did they?
3. **Denial of victim**—not really seeing a victim because the criminal distances him/herself from the victim or dehumanizes the victim in the mind due to their status. This is common for those who effect crimes on prostitutes or the homeless or have negative views of women they are intimately involved with.
4. **Condemnation of condemners**—rationalizing your behavior by basically saying that if those who are supposed to be obeying the law are not, or they are abusing their positions, then why should you be expected to be any better? When I hear of a corrupt politician or other public official in the news, my first thought is, how does that help the residents in that area who are trying to beat the odds and stay out of trouble?
5. **Appeal to higher authorities or loyalties**—when there is another set of rules governing the criminal that make the criminal behavior acceptable; for example, stealing or dealing drugs to gain money to provide for family members that are having economic struggles. However, being in dire need is not always a requirement for this technique. When I was in middle school, my first boyfriend stole a Christmas present for me (Beatles White Album). When he gave it to me and his friend told me how they had stolen it, my boyfriend was annoyed that I was upset

> and gave the gift back. I was not impressed. Bottom line, he was simply appealing to the higher authority and rule of boyfriends everywhere that it is important to get your girlfriend a gift, regardless of the method. And looking back, the expectation for an unemployed fourteen-year-old kid from a large family, who was not even supposed to be dating, to afford a gift was unreasonable. In today's society, this particular technique has wreaked havoc on many street criminals who are trying to get their lives back on track. Many want to get back in with their girlfriends or wives, or at the very least start a new relationship after time away from the opposite sex. But the reality is that for many men in today's society, especially those who are trying to uphold their sense of masculinity in more traditional relationships, the pressure to provide material items such as clothing, jewelry, and cars causes many to succumb to crime as a way to abide and appeal to the rules that govern relationships. This is a classic use of this final technique noted by Sykes and Matza.

Activity: Based on the above theory, come up with some topics of conversation you might have if you were a community correctional officer working for a probation department, parole department, or a prerelease program to try to change the thinking and rationalization of offenders who have an established criminal history involving either stealing cars, dealing drugs, or drunken brawls.

Summary

These theories are difficult to test, but they do make sense in understanding aspects of criminal behavior for which other theories fall short. These theories are also appealing to those who are open to the idea that criminals can change, given changes in their daily activities, associations, and mindsets. But it is not as easy as a simple conversation. The concepts of these theories need to be imbedded and practiced daily and monitored to assess the sincerity of an offender's involvement and change in thinking and rationalizations. This is much easier said than done. In fact, as much as the serial car thief was left speechless when I questioned why someone stealing my car caused him anger and concern, this moment of possible clarity was short-lived, and the young man returned to his criminal lifestyle within days of being released from the program. Thankfully, other theories help fill in some of the holes left by Sykes and Matza's drift concepts.

Social Control Theories

How is your desire to do the wrong or right thing controlled by others? How does the degree to which you can control yourself (i.e., self-control) contribute to the extent of your own criminal and deviant behavior? This second subcategory of process theories looks at how criminal behavior lies in the individual first but draws in the influence of informal social controls. However, the focus remains at the individual level.

Containment Theory

Walt Reckless (1973) is considered by many to be the father of social control theory. He is also regarded as a contributor to theories that focus on the underrated role of self-concept. In other words, the view you hold about yourself can determine how you respond to a situation and process through our society. What is a positive self-concept or positive self-esteem? In sum, it is an honest assessment of yourself by *yourself*, not by another person. While other people may help form your self-concept (an issue raised in upcoming theories), the bottom line is that we all have a sense of who we are when left to our own thoughts. And if these honest thoughts are not positive, with a decent dose of self-worth and pride, it can be easy to fall prey to the outside stressors of the environment, such as family dysfunction, poverty, tough neighborhoods, and so on. Reckless's theory asserts that it is our self-concept that contains and helps negotiate our way through life's struggles. And while positive outside influences may keep us out of harm's way, there are many who can still survive the negative aspects of life if their sense of self-worth and self-concept is intact. In essence, our self-concept serves as an insulator to help deflect whatever is coming at us from the outside.

Consider this containment theory analogy. If you were betting money on a race from Maine to California and had to choose the 2012 BMW SUV or the 1979 Chevrolet Nova with 100,000 miles as the winning vehicle, which vehicle would you pick? The most immediate obvious answer would be to go with the "beemer." But if you were smart, you might inquire about other factors before making your decision. A cross-country road trip is only as good as the drivers' abilities, temperaments, obsessions or lack thereof with texting and/or drinking while driving, and maybe even perhaps their knowledge about cars. Can they change a flat tire or oil, and can they navigate through various terrains? And yes, the BMW would probably be the better bet, just like in society, someone from a decent family, school, and neighborhood with no financial despair would be expected to steer clearer from the criminal justice system than their peer who has just the opposite set of external circumstances. But nothing is certain. Someone who grows up under unfavorable circumstances but feels good about themselves may triumph in the end. And coming from the "perfect" family, schools, and social strata is no guarantee that you will be even happy, let alone crime-free. Think about it. Look for it in the lives of the people you know. The next two theories discussed will elaborate further on these concepts. But Reckless gets credit for getting us to again think about another angle to approach the explanation of crime.

Social Control/Social Bond Theory

Travis Hirschi (1969) is a more commonly known name in introductory level sociology and criminal justice courses. Interestingly, his theory is one that remains in the textbooks despite its author's own disappointment in its limited explanation and lack of research support. However, this theory of social control does provide a level of insight that not only helps us understand why certain programs and policies in our society work or fail, it explains all types of deviance, from flunking a college course to committing serious crimes.

The most important aspect of social control theory is that it helps us to appreciate the value in asking why people are normal as opposed to why people are deviant. This was the line of questioning by Hirschi. I often find myself giving advice to friends regarding the topics of rocky marriages and raising troubled teens. And while often the conversations are centered on looking at all that is wrong in a particular marriage or the behaviors of a wayward and rebellious teen, at times the discussions focus on inquiring about what the "secrets" are to my marriage or the upbringing of my relatively "normal" children.

So, in pursuing this line of inquiry, Hirschi resolved the following: We all lean toward deviance. No marriage or child is perfect. The temptation to deviate is part of the human experience. However, what he observed in developing his social control theory was that people who were strongly bonded to conventional society were more "normal." Specifically, they were connected through the following bonds:

- **Attachment** (having the bonds in the first place)
- **Involvement** (spending time in the bond activities)
- **Commitment** (personal investment)
- **Belief** in the validity of societal rules and laws

On the contrary, crime and deviance are explained by weak bonds. These four bonds are important to understand both separately and together because being attached to something is not the same as personal involvement or commitment, which requires a sense of personal investment. Finally, if you do not believe in what you are doing or, in the case of crime, if you do not believe in the validity of the rule of law, it will undermine the extent of your bond. Criminals who are not well bonded may look from the outside like they are on the road to recovery because they are incarcerated, or in a rehab center or drug court, and have decided to rejoin their family circles. However, showing up is just a piece of the bond. If the underlying commitment is not there, combined with the belief system, failure is inevitable.

Consider the following illustration of this theory in a noncriminal context. One semester, I had a student who flunked an introductory sociology course, even though he had perfect attendance in a class that met three times per week. After he had flunked the first two exams and turned in a hand-written essay entitled "Marijuana is a Brown Leafy Substance," which also came complete with the fragrant aroma of THC, I kindly advised the student as final exams were approaching that he was likely not going to pass the course. He did not seem that surprised or disturbed and continued to attend class and even showed up for the final. When I looked at his final essay exam and realized it was a nice letter wishing my family a nice holiday season, I chased after him and inquired in a nonhostile, yet inquisitive manner, "What is your deal?" He then went on to explain that while he thought I was a "nice lady and all" and that some of the lectures were interesting, he had no intention of returning to college, and the only reason he enrolled was because his parents gave him an ultimatum: move out and get a job, or enroll in community college. With this also came the understanding that if he failed to attend a single class, he would be kicked out of the house. He also explained that the reason he would not be returning was because he had a job and apartment lined up, but that he was simply too lazy and not ready to work and live on his own back when the semester started. And finally, the most critical point he made was that he did not believe in the institution of higher education and that he felt it was basically a big rip-off and that he could easily skip this step and still be a success in society. Bingo! Got it! The main point of this example is to illustrate that simply being attached to a conventional activity in society, such as college, is not enough to provide success. We all know students who have what I call "bounced out" of four-year institutions due to some combination of failing grades, binge drinking, drug problems, or even legal issues. The bottom line is that the attachment bond is not enough. This theory helps explain a lot of criminal and noncriminal deviance in our society. Practitioners are often discouraged by the mediocre success rates of various programs aimed at helping criminals return to conventional society and its values, but this theory shows that this is easier said than done and all four bonds must be appreciated and incorporated fully into any plan or efforts to change behavior.

Low Self-Control Theory

The last social control theory mentioned for this category is a theory that Hirschi developed due to his critique of his aforementioned social control theory, given its limits in explaining what impacts bonding to conventional society. Along with Michael Gottfredson (1990), Hirschi recognized that there are certain personality characteristics that seem more prevalent among criminals that might make certain types of criminal activity more attractive to some individuals. That personal trait is low self-control. Now, we can probably all come up with examples of people in our lives who exhibit low self-control by their impulsivity, need for instant gratification, and/or risky behavior. This theory is relatively new and takes us in a different direction. In developing this theory, Gottfredson and Hirschi analyzed a variety of behaviors that exemplified self-control problems. The three main behaviors, which are in large part noncriminal, were gambling, unprotected sex, and adultery (cheating). What do these behaviors have in common? The answer is that they are risky. Gottfredson and Hirschi explored the types of character traits that go along with these types of people who might engage in any or all of these behaviors. Clearly, these behaviors are impulsive, selfish, and insensitive, and the individuals do not have the best patience or self-control. From this, Gottfredson and Hirschi then asked the question, how does one develop poor self-control? Why do some people engage in criminal and noncriminal deviance that is so impulsive? Although the answer is not clear-cut, initial discussions focus on the role of parenting. This is due in part to the fact that we know from the field of psychology and sociology that much of our personality is for the most part crystallized by about age eight. And while schools are an agent of socialization during this time, it is what goes on in the household that mostly molds our sense of self. The issue of parenting is very sensitive and requires additional testing. Parenting is difficult to study, especially during formative ages. But one observation made through this theory is that parents who are inconsistent, neglectful, and/or too authoritative negatively influence their children and are more likely to add to the development of low self-control as a personality trait. On the contrary, parents that are more proactive and supervisory in nature, don't "blow up" at their children, and are more involved in the various areas of their children's lives help strengthen the traits of impulse control and selflessness that stand contrary to low self-control.

Control Balance Theory: An Integrated Approach to Understanding Control

The above theories have been provided to illustrate the more prominent social control theories. However, a closer and more literal examination of how "control" influences individual decisions regarding certain criminal behaviors is worth considering. While recognized mostly as an integrated theory for criminal and noncriminal deviance and drawing on many of the categorical themes illustrated through neo-classical and process theories, Charles Tittle's Control Balance Theory provides another lens to examine crime. For the sake of brevity, below is a summary of Tittle's 1995 integrated theory incorporating his 2004 revisions as it may apply to understanding criminal deviance.

At the heart of control balance theory is the observation that individuals who do not have a healthy balance of control in their daily lives (i.e., control deficits) are predisposed to accommodating for their deficits or surplus through their criminal behavior. Additionally, according to Tittle (2004), decisions to engage in crime may be affected by how one perceives the long-term benefit, and whether the act is "impersonal." This impersonality can impact the decision-making process by distancing the offender from the victim as discussed previously in this chapter through the techniques of neutralization.

Control Deficit Examples

Power Control Surplus: Someone who has a job with a lot of power such as overseeing a major corporation or the chief of police, has an amount of power that surpasses the normal individual. In order to preserve this power, he/she may react hostilely to family members or coworkers perceived as a threat to the power they have come to expect.

Power Control Deficit: An individual who works in the lower rungs of a corporation and experiences a general sense of having little to no control over decisions made in their socio-economic life is more likely to commit employee theft as a way to manage their deficit with the impersonal nature of this type of crime, making it easier to rationalize.

Control Balance Theory and Self-Control

You may be wondering if this theory should be taken to mean that all people with control deficits are predisposed to the same type of deviance? The short answer is no. Tittle (2004) makes a point of realizing that some people who experience these deficits act more irrationally than others. Keeping in mind, crime can occur both rationally and irrationally. For example a carefully planned scheme to steal from a corporation versus launching yourself at another person during a heated argument, resulting in a serious assault or even worse, a homicide illustrates this distinction. So, what is the difference? One of the key issues, which was also raised earlier in this chapter through low-self-control theory, is just that, the level of self-control one carries. In his initial development of this theory Tittle introduced the notion of one's control ratio as being key.

Control Ratio: The extent to which an individual can potentially exercise control over circumstances impinging on him, relative to the potential control that can be exercised by external entities and conditions against the individual.

Additional Considerations

Control balance theory is complex as individual lives are affected by various diversity and experiential factors. The following five converging factors noted by Tittle reveal why this theory is commonly referred to as an integrated approach:

1. A predisposition toward being motivated for deviance
2. Situational provocation that reminds a person of a control imbalance
3. Transformation of predisposition to actual motivation
4. Opportunity
5. Absence or weak constraints impacting perception of gain in control

Labeling Theories (Societal Reactions Theory)

How does what other people think about the things you have done and the different ways they react to your criminal and delinquent behavior influence your future behavior? Does it make sense to also consider how reactions to our good behavior in the context of our criminal behavior play a role in reducing or promoting future criminal behavior?

This final category of process theories has had many contributors over the years. Many students have been introduced to Charles Cooley's (1902) looking-glass self, or the self-fulfilling prophecy, and/or the interactionist perspective. A central theme of this concept and perspective is that much of who we are is a result of how we have been treated and how we are viewed by others. The claim is that we rely on the reactions of others to help develop our sense of self. There are many who have contributed to the general premise of labeling theory; however, I have provided an analogy below to help students understand the basic principles of labeling theory. Then, by introducing John Braithwaite's Reintegrative Shaming Theory (1989) and Lawrence Sherman's Defiance Theory (1993), students can see how the general principles of labeling theory have been used to continue developing applications.

Labeling Theory (Overview)

A central theme of labeling theory is that the degree of our continued criminality depends on how formal agencies react to us upon our first "offense." Discretion in the system among law enforcement, judges, school administrators, and so on allow for varying degrees of responses to behaviors. Just as they depend on the house you grew up in, response to behaviors may range from no reaction to moderate reaction such as grounding, or even being kicked out of one's house. Not every teenager who uses foul language, smokes marijuana, and comes home with failing grades will get the same response. Some parents will respond with a level of concern, perhaps therapy, or just a series of conversations with family and the school, whereas in other households the child is punished, maybe even shunned. Labeling theory asks the question, which response is best? It is all about the reaction. The premise of labeling theory is that if one's behavior is overreacted to, then the person having to manage the reaction is more likely to continue in the deviant and criminal ways because the negative stigmas and negative emotions associated with being shamed are internalized and then become part of that person's reality. Central to labeling theory is that we are constantly interpreting the interactions we have with others, and we use those interpretations to help define who we are.

Implied in labeling theory is that labels come with varying degrees of stickiness. Think of how effective the labeling methods for a child's clothes for summer camp would be if you used post-it sticky notes as labels. Now compare this with sewing in a label with your child's name, address, and phone number into each item of clothing. When this analogy is applied to criminals, it is assumed as well that the less sticky the label, the less likely it will stay on the criminal. Therefore, the reactions we have to criminals, especially during teenage years, when we are really relying on others to help define our sense of self, is key.

When my son was in the fifth grade, he came home from school with a two-day detention slip for being "disrespectful" on the shuttle bus carrying students in grades five through eight. During a reprimand of an older student, my son and his friend were uncomfortable with witnessing this type of reprimand, and so they fidgeted and laughed. They were warned, and my son was still unable to remain silent. He was then marched to the principal's office, where he apologized for his behavior and was then sent home with his detention slip. Now first of all, let me say that, in my view, there is no place for detention in fifth grade! Educators must be more creative and interested in our children than to put these labels out at this age. After speaking with my son, I contacted the school. I was not only concerned about the impact on my son of having detention, I was also aware that the school practiced putting all students' names who were in trouble on the front board in the classroom, and they would call students down to the detention room over the loudspeaker system just before dismissal. My concerns about labeling were obvious. The administrator explained to me that ordinarily this type of offense would have warranted being suspended from recess; however, given the cold New England temperatures that week, outdoor recess was not an option, so that the punishment would be detention. After questioning this rationale and comparing it with essentially giving the death penalty for prisoners serving life sentences due to overcrowding, the administrator compromised and reduced the punishment to a one-day partial detention. But, and a big but, the most important conversation I had that day was not with the school administrators; rather, it was with my son. He needed to understand that given his age and the reputation that follows kids who are labeled as troublemakers, he was going to have to be aware and work to ensure that this label did not stay with him. And I am proud to say, knock on wood, that there have been no disciplinary problems with my son since. A parent with no knowledge of labeling might have taken a very different tact, resulting in reinforcement of the label, and ultimately the child's embracing of it.

Reintegrative Shaming Theory

Labeling theory offers a lot of insight into human behavior. John Braithwaite (1989) has taken special interest in the formal control of the criminal justice system and how it has historically used negative shaming and labeling throughout the criminal justice process. This type of shaming is referred to as **disintegrative**. This shaming holds all the qualities noted above in labeling theory and produces negative feelings of shame, embarrassment, and guilt, which over time can make a criminal fulfill that label and continue to engage in criminal behavior as that label requires. To illustrate this point, think about a typical drug bust where the government is well prepared and ready to effect an arrest and search warrant on a multicount, multidefendant drug case. The likely scenario is that agents will arrive at the residence in the wee hours of the morning. They will enter dynamically, and if the suspects are asleep or in the bathroom, they will find themselves handcuffed and lying on the floor, perhaps not even fully dressed, as agents search their residence. If family members, including children, are there, the scene will be all the more chaotic. And if neighbors are around and television crews have been alerted, the labeling process will begin—with force. And all the way through the criminal justice process, whether it be the intake at the jail, being searched, being photographed, or appearing in a public court, local newspaper, or nightly newscast, this defendant will have many, many reminders of their criminal behavior and ample opportunity to experience disintegrative shame. And even if fortunate enough to receive a probationary sentence, submitting to public urinalysis, reporting to a probation officer, and having home visits are all ways he or she will experience the labeling process.

Braithwaite, however, has suggested that the system embrace another form of shaming, namely **reintegrative shaming**, which is a way to recognize some of the other labels held by defendants that are outside of their criminality. Have you ever heard of a probation or parole hearing for violators? Of course. But have you ever heard of a court hearing for an offender's successful completion of probation or parole, during which time their education, employment, familial and other social accomplishments, such as getting clean and sober, are acknowledged publicly and announced in local papers and newscasts? Probably not. But the idea behind reintegrative shaming theory is that by using hearings and other interventions that recognize and draw attention to additional labels, we can reduce the impact and the stickiness of the negative, criminal label. The ultimate goal is to shed the criminal label and replace it with positive ones such as student, parent, sibling, employee, and so on. This theory in practice is evidenced in restorative justice programs, which have gained popularity since the mid-1990s. However, in an ultra-conservative political climate, and also among most citizens, who aren't well versed in theory, spending time, money, and energy in this way is not an easy sell. But it is worth considering. Some of the documentaries and stories reviewed in this course will reveal evidence that this alternative approach to addressing crime is worth a look.

Defiance Theory

Another theory aimed at critically assessing the significance of the labeling process is defiance theory. Lawrence Sherman (1993), highlights that there is some merit in appreciating the conclusions drawn by the neo-classical theories and their emphasis on punishment as a way to reduce crime. More specifically, looking at the quality of the sanction and the differences among offenders may assist in understanding the delicate balance of punishment and behavior control. This theory also brings up the element of respect that is directly addressed in subculture theory, but certainly applies and should be considered among labeling theories.

The term defiance is used theoretically to refer to the net increase in future criminal or delinquent behavior because of the labeling process that is fueled by the response and attitude of the individual toward those dispensing the punishment. There are two types of defiance, specific and general. **Specific defiance** occurs when the offender is reacting to their own punishment. **General defiance** occurs when others act out as a group due to the punishment of someone from their in-group or subculture. The type of reoffending can vary from being directly aimed at the individual deemed responsible for the actual punishment, or toward a sanctioning agent they believe represents the unjustifiable punishment. A critical part to this theory is when those punished or observing the punishment of their in-group define the sanction as being unfair. Sanctions are unfair under two main conditions: the sanctioning agent disrespects the offender or their in-group, regardless of how fair the sanction is, and/or the sanction is substantively discriminatory, arbitrary, undeserved, or excessive. When this happens, according to this theory the offender may deny the shameful feelings and respond by internalizing rage and labeling the sanctioning agent as the one deserving punishment. The degree of a negative and criminal response is aggravated when the offender already has weak bonds or feels alienated by the sanctioning agent or who and what they stand for.

This theory assists in understanding the tension in our inner cities and poor minority-police relations. Studies have well documented this, and some have noted what is referred to as a "shame-disrespect-anger spiral" among police and poor young men (Scheff and Retzinger, 1991, p. 68). A term that has evolved from this theory is **substantive unfairness**, which refers to the dynamic that occurs when an alleged offender approaches authority with a defiant attitude and they are often punished for their speech rather than the initial offense. The term "contempt of cop" has been coined over the years to illustrate the nature of these oppositional interactions. A final note, the concept of *perceived* disrespect has been shown to be a factor, especially when one is directly experiencing the sanctioning.

Activity: Create a scenario regarding an encounter between an offender and either a police officer, probation officer, correctional officer or judge that might explain continued criminal behavior according to labeling theories.

Chapter 6

Conflict Theories

How does living in a society that is inherently unequal, where our life chances are in part influenced by our social class, gender, and race or ethnic subculture impact how we are treated, perceived, labeled, and punished for our criminal behavior? How does recognizing this inequality lead to greater equal protection under the law, understanding, and more effective policies and interventions?

Conflict theory evolved out of the social context of harsh punishment and a state of retribution that the United States has embraced since the 1970s. Conflict theory is often referred to as *critical criminology,* as it examines the inner workings of the system with the ideas in mind that it might not be working as fairly and successfully as it should, and that certain groups in society have not been given the proper attention deserved in the study of criminal behavior because they do not hold power in a society that is stratified. Conflict theorists are bold to ask difficult and oftentimes uncomfortable questions that center around controversial topics. For example, suggesting that racial profiling exists and has a direct and indirect impact on our perception of crime, is a much needed, but often avoided, conversation in classrooms, households, and mass media. It usually takes a high-profile news event tragedy to jar our attention. And even then, the discussions are muddled and overtaken with the high emotional stakes that people have based on their own personal experiences and political ideologies.

Today, most students of criminal justice and criminology will take a course that focuses on the unique issues that this broad category introduces. For the purpose of understanding the basic premise of conflict theory and some of the sub-categories of theories within, the following terms and concepts are introduced:

Sources of Power

The three main sources of power in our society that are used to further the interests of those deemed powerful at the expense of those deemed less powerful are:

- Race/ethnicity
- Economics (Micro and Macro)
- Gender

A Hispanic working class female does not hold the most power in our society. There are other ways that power is distributed as well, such as through sexual orientation, immigration status, religion, and nationality; however, these three sources are the most commonly identified as troublesome in a democratic society where justice is supposed to be equally distributed.

Within conflict theory, often theorists will focus on either multiple sources of power that convene upon society leading to inequality, or at times one of the particular sources of power that is believed by some to be the true culprit will. Radical and feminist theories are examples of offshoots of conflict theory that spend more time analyzing the critical issues of our economic system (radical theory) and the role of gender (feminist theory).

Concepts and Terms

Racial Threat Hypothesis

This hypothesis that asserts that as a minority group grows in number relative to the majority group (that being the group in power), more laws and/or punishment aimed at the minority group will be created and/or enhanced. This hypothesis reveals the very basic premise of conflict theory. It is an idea that has been used to analyze the fairness of crack cocaine laws of the 1980s, which targeted inner city poor blacks. Also, it lends to our understanding of why some of the most prevalent drug problems today, such as the abuse of prescription pain killers in predominantly white working and middle class suburban communities, are not being addressed with the same vigor as the crack cocaine epidemic. Based on your understanding of conflict theory, what would the level of inquiry involve for either of these situations? Is the suggestion that what has since been ruled by the United States Sentencing Commission (USSC) to be an overly harsh response to crack cocaine in the 80s, and the lack of harsh response to prescription drug use today, impacted by race? In other words, were white powder cocaine users in the 80s protected like many white prescription opiate and meth users today? Were whites unfairly able to avoid becoming involved in the criminal justice system and being susceptible to lengthy incarceration, or at the very least accusation and confrontation by the legal system?

(See report on pgs. 69–72)

One of the key components to Conflict theory is the premise that only by admitting inequality can society make an effort to achieve equality. Consider this brief excerpt on recent actions taken in 2010 which have ongoing impact in reducing the sentences for qualifying federal inmates serving time for crack cocaine offenses. Note: This discussion helps remind us that *law makers* are one of the three essential areas of study in this field.

June 21, 2012. Supreme Court Crack Cocaine Decision: A Vote for Justice

Marc Mauer, Executive Director of The Sentencing Project, commented on the June 21 decision by the U.S. Supreme Court in the cases of *Dorsey v. United States* and *Hill v. United States*:

Today's decision represents a vote for fairness and justice. Congress passed the Fair Sentencing Act in 2010 as a recognition of the unfair and excessively punitive nature of federal crack cocaine sentencing. To continue to sentence defendants under provisions that are now universally seen as antiquated would only serve to perpetuate this longstanding injustice.

He added

The racial disparities created by federal crack cocaine sentencing were profound, with African Americans constituting 80% of defendants. Today's decision marks another step toward racial fairness.[1]

1 link: http://www.sentencingproject.org/detail/news.cfm?new_id=1319

What is important to recognize about conflict theories is that their questions are controversial and there is always going to be another side to the story, point of view, or set of questions posed by those in power or by those simply seeking the truth. For example, one might suggest that the reason that our prison system is disproportionally black is because the crimes committed by blacks (currently close to 50% of all homicides) are going to be subject to harsher penalties. This observation recognizes the role of what is commonly referred to as ***legal factors***. In sentencing serious criminal offenses in this country, two key factors are the focus: the crime committed and the criminal history (including arrest, past incarceration, and convictions). These types of legal factors may also provide insight into what appears to be unfairness but may really just be coincidence, albeit unfortunate, that exists among certain demographic populations. However, the role of ***extra-legal factors*** must as be also considered. Extra Legal factors include, but are not limited to, the roles of neighborhood, family, school, exposure to police, and many of the factors noted by structure and labeling theorists that might in part explain not just criminal behavior, but the chances that one is more likely to be dealt with formally by the criminal justice system.

Activity: To assure understanding of the essential premise of the Racial Threat Hypothesis, consider the current issue and controversies surrounding immigration policy changes in the U.S. What questions might a conflict theorist pose?

Radical Theory

Radical theory directs our attention to the unequal distribution of wealth and power as well as our economic system of capitalism. It explores the many ways a supply and demand culture support the idea that many criminals are no different perhaps than car salespersons, liquor store owners, or a convenience store that sells lottery tickets. Capitalism implies that if you have a desirable skill or a product, you should be able to market that skill set and be compensated accordingly. For example, any profession, whether it be teaching, garbage collecting, or selling trinkets in an airport, is affected by supply and demand forces. This is also true, then, for the drug dealer, fencer of stolen goods, and prostitute, etc. Therefore, one area of pursuit for the radical theorist is to look at how living in a capitalist society instills at some level a criminal mindset. Structure theory gives us some insight into how capitalism and the pressure to succeed contribute to crime. Radical theory also looks at how capitalism in the U.S. promotes great social inequality and the impact that living at the bottom may have in driving some towards crime. Also, the pressure to maintain positions at the top is considered. In other words, those living at the top may commit crimes when their positions are in jeopardy. Just take a look at recent events surrounding white collar criminals.

Compassionate Capitalism

A final component to radical theory worth mentioning is what solutions are offered as a way to reduce crime in a society that will mostly forever be steeped in capitalist values, incentives, and norms. One term I have come across to illustrate a possible solution is ***compassionate capitalism***, coined in 2004 by Mark Benioff and Karen Southwick. What is compassionate capitalism? In sum, compassionate capitalism is an economic system that recognizes the importance of free enterprise and private ownership but also acknowledges the importance of caring for all individuals, especially those who may not be able to benefit fully from this system. These individuals are at risk. They may commit crime or engage in self-defeating behavior. Compassionate capitalism acknowledges that some individuals struggle in a free market society and that within reason they deserve to be supported. And while that support may be at a cost to society at large, it far outweighs the financial and societal costs of crime.

To conclude, let me leave you with a true case scenario that helps illustrate what is meant by compassionate capitalism. When I was employed as a federal probation officer in 1991, I had heard about what is commonly known as the FMLA (Family and Medical Leave Act), which, so I thought, would provide me with no less than three full months of paid maternity leave when I was ready to have a child. I was also under the impression that in certain cases I might be allowed up to six months of maternity leave, and while it might not be paid, if I planned accordingly, I would be able to return to my job. During my sixth month of pregnancy in 1992, I was provided with a rude awaking by the human resources department, which was that the three months of paid leave and a guaranteed job upon my return would only work if I had accumulated enough sick leave and vacation time to cover the three months. Obviously, this was not the case. And given that I was the breadwinner at the time and launching into a career, my husband and I were in no position to change our circumstances. So after going to work every day regardless of how tired or uncomfortable I felt, and then returning to work after just five weeks at home with my first child, I realized that what appeared to sound like a "compassionate" approach to helping me maintain my job, as well as enjoy my maternity leave, was really not that compassionate at all. Fortunately, my husband was willing and obviously capable of spending several months at home with our infant daughter as I returned to my full-time job, which at the time was our main source of income, insurance, and stability. Hmmmmm ... does that sound compassionate to you? Now imagine this type of financial, familial, or health stressor placed on those with different options and resources. Criminal activity may be one of the options, whether it be at an individual level or through collective behaviors such as the "occupy movements" that have been popularized during these economic times. While this theory does not stand alone to explain all crime, it is another aspect to look at. When combined with some of the other theoretical aspects it can add to a better understanding of the complexity of many forms of criminal behavior.

Feminist Theory

To many sociologists, feminist theory is part of the conflict perspective that evolved within the field of sociology to show how inequalities in our society must be recognized in order to make progress towards equality and change. From this perspective, there are many within the field of criminology who focus on gender with specific attention on how being male in our society is a tool of power. Feminist theory also recognizes that women have been understudied in the field of crime theory, as a majority of the theorists (in fact all mentioned in the chapters preceding this one) have been male. One of the unintentional outcomes has been an underappreciation of the uniqueness of both female criminals and victims. Feminist theory also reminds us that in an androcentric society, our major institutions such as family, religion, politics, and the criminal justice system have added to a type of gender socialization that runs the risk of placing women in circumstances where they find themselves being treated differently.

The gender role socialization process, while ever-changing, still molds and in some cases dictates the way women should act and be treated in a myriad of social situations. Consider the following hypothesis statements included in a well-respected journal article by Karen Heimer and Stacy DeCoster (1999):

- "Boys will learn more violent definitions than girls in part because boys are subject to lower levels of familial control than girls, have more aggressive friends than girls, and have more experience with prior violence than girls."
- "Learning traditional gender definitions will reduce the chances of violent delinquency among females and increase the chances of violent delinquency among males."

Feminist theory is a significant category of crime theory for which a survey of crime theories cannot do justice. Today, most criminal justice programs require, or at the very least offer, courses that focus on the specific issue of gender as well as other sources of power already identified. There is also a range of approaches to feminist theory. Some focus on women as victims, others as offenders; some focus on how the criminal justice system has treated women, young and old, and how the inconsistent treatment may be beneficial and/or detrimental. Feminist theory has also produced a genre of highly respected research and criminologists who have shed light on the issue of women and crime. One such criminologist is Nicole Hahn Rafter (1991, 2006d), who shed light on not only the sociological, but the biological and psychological considerations in furthering a deeper understanding of how women are viewed, treated, and processed in the criminal justice system. Consider the importance and implications of Rafter's early work on women and incarceration.

> Until recently, women's institutions and their inmates have received little attention in the literature on prisons. This neglect in part stems from the fact that over time women have comprised but a small fraction of the total prisoner population. Yet it is also the product of two common assumptions: that the development of the women's prison system and experiences of its inmates closely resemble those of men; or that, if different, the evolution of the women's prison system and female experience of incarceration are irrelevant to mainstream penology just because they can shed little light on the nature of the prison system as a whole. Neither assumption is correct. During the first stage in the development of the women's prison system (1790–1870), female penal units outwardly resembled male penitentiaries, but in some respects their inmates received inferior care. During the second stage (1870–1935), strenuous and often successful efforts were made to establish an entirely new type of prison, the women's reformatory, in which women would receive care more appropriate to their "feminine" nature. (Hahn Rafter, 1983)

Below are additional illustrations of how feminist theory has contributed to a deeper understanding of crime.

1. ***The liberation hypothesis***—a term first coined by Freda Adler (1975), suggests that as women have been liberated in the legitimate world, so too will they be liberated in the criminal world. Careful not to blame the women's movement for an increase in crime, this hypothesis provides a general framework for considering the increase of women in crimes traditionally committed by men (i.e. white-collar crime, drug dealing, gang activity).
2. ***Typologies of female offenders***—one way to study women and crime is to review the various reasons and factors that are found in the lives of women who are involved in the criminal justice system as offenders. Criminologist Kathleen Daly (1994) did just that by analyzing the pre-sentence investigation reports of female offenders. From this she was able to develop typologies showing that female offenders differ from their male counterparts such as the **battered and battering woman, the abused and abusing woman, and the drug connected woman.** While the study is not fully revealed here, it is noteworthy as it shows that it is worthwhile to study

female offenders; she found that many had issues in their backgrounds such as abuse, past and present, and situational circumstances that brought them into their criminality. One typology is what she describes as the **drug-connected woman**. In her studies, she found that some women of today, unlike women prior to the mid-1980s, are not only involved with men who are involved in the drug trade, but are entrusted with roles in the conspiracy, most often as courier. Some of these scenarios have undertones of abuse, as their "men," whether they be husbands, boyfriends, or in some cases siblings or children, exploit women and put them in the most dangerous scenarios of getting caught and/or harmed, while most of the proceeds are still going to the men they are connected to. During my years as a federal probation officer, I recall one drug case that fit this scenario. The defendant's attorney raised an interesting point during the pre-sentence investigation, which was that his client was not only part of the drug dealing, but she was being abused by her drug-dealing boyfriend. Upon investigation, it was determined that her story was credible. Does this mean that she should not be held criminally liable for her part in a drug distribution conspiracy? In this case, absolutely not. In fact, the United States Sentencing Commission had already been confronted with this scenario, and it had incorporated it into in its formulation in the then-widely respected and used federal sentencing guidelines. It was determined that this type of scenario would be best addressed as a mitigating circumstance at the time of sentencing. This scenario leads to the third observation I'd like to make that illustrates the invaluable contributions of feminist theories, and that is the role of chivalry in the criminal justice system.

3. ***Is chivalry dead?*** Do we live in a day where being a woman does not come with the assumption that doors will be opened for us, dates will be paid for, and when it comes to crime and justice, that women will be protected? This question is one that is raised by the feminist theorists, and it is one for which there is no clear answer. Depending on the crime, the time, and in many cases the region of our country, as well as considering other diversity factors such as race and age, it could be concluded that women have been treated less harshly over the years. After all, the 75:25 ratio of male: female crime and the approximate 90:10 ratio of male:female incarceration seems to support that women are treated favorably. One of the most glaring cases that highlights this issue was that of a female drug courier, who could be described as the classic drug-connected woman. By the time she was ready to change her plea to guilty, her co-defendant had pled guilty and was already incarcerated, and she was caring for an infant son she had with her co-defendant as well as a ten-year-old child from a previous relationship. Part of her offense conduct was to hide heroin in her car, often using car seats and other items associated with her children as a decoy. Upon arriving to court, I inquired with her attorney to be sure that she had made arrangements for someone to care for her children, as given the rebuttable presumption of mandatory detention prior to sentencing law for most convicted drug offenders, she was going to be

detained. The defense attorney, who was highly paid but lowly familiar with the inner workings of the federal system, tried to hide his surprise at my inquiry. He advised that things were all set and that he fully expected his client to be released following her entrance of the guilty plea. After all, she was the primary caregiver of two young children. Twenty minutes later, he watched his client get cuffed by the U.S. Marshals in front of her two children and her wailing mother as she was placed in custody. Despite counsel's efforts to convince the judge that this woman and mother needed to be out pending sentencing to care for her children, the judge firmly stated that for the court to be asked now to care about this dilemma more than she did when she decided to engage in illegal activity was absurd. In this case, chivalry was dead!

Activity/Reflection: Consider the current "Me Too" social movement. What questions would Feminist Theory pose? What are some explanation that Feminist Theory might suggest help understand both why this type of crime happens?

Further test your comprehension of conflict theory and consider that while this social movement was established in 2006 by Tarana Burke, a black activist, who founded the movement to help survivors of sexual violence, particularly young women of color from low wealth communities, it has not been well known until more recently (i.e., #MeToo), promoted in large part by alleged victims out of the Hollywood movie industry.

Summary

Conflict theories force us to take a look at some difficult and controversial issues facing our criminal justice system. With regards to explaining why crime occurs, they suggest that sometimes the answer lies in the system and laws, our economic structure, and our culture. These aspects often overlap and deserve the attention of research and educators of those who are going to be employed in the system. While the answers are not 100% clear and controversy is inevitable given the challenge of studying such a vast decentralized system, they are worth pursuit. One of the roots for conflict theory as a sociological domain is that in order to make change towards equality, we need to appreciate and acknowledge inequality. The contributions of conflict theory in making strides in reducing intimate partner abuse, domestic violence, unfair racial profiling practices, and the evolution of our laws, to name just a few, are proof that conflict theory is here to stay. So, go ahead, ask the uncomfortable questions, learn about how race, social class, our economy, and gender impact crime and justice issues. You certainly are not alone.

Activity/Reflection: Spend a few moments to reflect on current events, news stories that have made you question whether discrimination and bias might have played a role in the outcome. The apprehension, prosecution, and punishment of criminals in the United States should not be impacted by race, ethnicity, social class, and/or gender if equal protection under the law is a constitutional right we wish to uphold. But is this the case?

Below is a historical account of the crack cocaine disparity referenced earlier in this chapter:

Sentencing Policy: Unjustified and Unreasonable

Overview

Crack cocaine became prevalent in the mid-1980s and received massive media attention due in part to the death of college basketball star Len Bias (subsequently found to have used powder cocaine on the night of his death and not crack). Crack was portrayed as a violence inducing, highly addictive plague of inner cities, and this media spotlight led to the quick passage of two federal sentencing laws concerning crack cocaine in 1986 and 1988. The laws created a 100:1 quantity ratio between the amount of crack and powder cocaine needed to trigger certain mandatory minimum sentences for trafficking, as well as creating a mandatory minimum penalty for simple possession of crack cocaine. The result of these laws is that crack users and dealers receive much harsher penalties than users and dealers of powder cocaine.

The Difference between Crack and Cocaine Powder

Cocaine powder is derived from coca paste, which is in turn derived from the leaves of the coca plant. Crack cocaine is made by taking cocaine powder and cooking it with baking soda and water until it forms a hard substance. These "rocks" can then be broken into pieces and sold in small quantities. Each gram of powder produces approximately .89 grams of crack.

The psychotropic and physiological effects of all types of cocaine are the same, but the intensity and duration of the high differ according to the route of administration. Crack is always smoked and gives a fast, intense high. Powder cocaine is usually snorted, which gives a slower and less intense high. Supporters of the 100:1 quantity ratio say that the intensity of the high created by crack makes crack more addictive than powder and makes its users more violence prone. Experts believe that crack is more likely to be abused because the high is short, which causes users to desire more of the drug, and because it is cheap and widely available. But when powder cocaine is injected it produces a fast, intense high similar to crack.

The United States Sentencing Commission (USSC) was created by Congress in 1984 to develop federal sentencing guidelines that would, among other goals, reduce unwarranted sentencing disparity. In 1995 the Commission concluded that the violence associated with crack is primarily related to the drug trade and not to the effects of the drug itself.[2] Crack is inexpensive and usually sold in small quantities, so it is often sold in open-air markets which are especially prone to violence. Powder is also distributed in this manner, but it is usually sold in larger wholesale quantities behind closed doors—in locations which

2 United States Sentencing Commission, Special Report to Congress: Cocaine and Federal Sentencing Policy (Washington, D.C.: GPO, February 1995), 184–187.

are inherently more secure. Both powder and crack cocaine cause distribution-related violence, but crack is more often sold in volatile settings.

Sentencing Policy

Although the two types of cocaine cause similar physical reactions, the sentences that users and sellers of the drugs face are vastly different. For powder cocaine, a conviction of possession with intent to distribute carries a five year sentence for quantities of 500 grams or more. But for crack, a conviction of possession with intent to distribute carries a five-year sentence for only 5 grams. This is a 100:1 quantity ratio. Under this format, a dealer charged with trafficking 400 grams of powder, worth approximately $40,000, could receive a shorter sentence than a user he supplied with crack valued at $500. Crack is also the only drug that carries a mandatory prison sentence for first offense possession. A person convicted in federal court of possession of 5 grams of crack automatically receives a 5-year prison term. A person convicted of possessing 5 grams of powder cocaine will probably receive a probation sentence. The maximum sentence for simple possession of any other drug, including powder cocaine, is 1 year in jail.

In addition to the federal mandatory minimum sentences, 14 states differentiate between crack and powder cocaine. However, none have a quantity ratio as large as the 100:1 disparity in federal law.

Racial Disparity

Approximately 2/3 of crack users are white or Hispanic, yet the clear majority of persons convicted of possession in federal courts in 1994 were African American, according to the USSC. Defendants convicted of crack possession in 1994 were 84.5% black, 10.3% white, and 5.2% Hispanic. Trafficking offenders were 4.1% white, 88.3% black, and 7.1% Hispanic. Powder cocaine offenders were more racially mixed. Defendants convicted of simple possession of cocaine powder were 58% white, 26.7% black, and 15% Hispanic. The powder trafficking offenders were 32% white, 27.4% black, and 39.3% Hispanic. The result of the combined difference in sentencing laws and racial disparity is that black men and women are serving longer prison sentences than white men and women.

Legislative History

In 1986 and 1988 Congress adopted mandatory sentencing laws on crack in the wake of widespread media attention. These laws were based on the idea that crack is "50 times more addictive" than powder cocaine. Congress doubled that number and came up with the 100:1 quantity ratio currently in effect.[3] As part of the 1994 Omnibus Violent Crime Control and Law Enforcement Act, the U.S. Sentencing Commission was directed to study the differing penalties for powder and crack cocaine. In 1995, the commission recommended equalizing the quantity ratio that would trigger the mandatory sentences. They also pointed out that the Federal Sentencing Guidelines provide criteria other than drug type to determine sentence lengths, so that violent, dangerous dealers receive

3 Gary Webb, "Flawed Sentencing the main reason for race disparity," *Mercury News*, 20 Aug 1996.

longer sentences. Congress rejected the recommendation, which marked the first time it had done so since the establishment of the Sentencing Commission. The President then followed Congress and signed the rejection into law.

Litigation

The 100:1 quantity ratio in the federal system has been legally challenged as unconstitutional on the grounds that it denies equal protection or due process, because the penalties constitute cruel and unusual punishment, and because the statutes are unconstitutionally vague. All of these challenges have failed in the federal appellate courts. However, in a state case regarding a statute that enhanced crack cocaine penalties at a 10:3 ratio, the Minnesota Supreme Court struck down the enhancement based on the more expansive equal protection guarantees of its state constitution.[4]

In the case *United States v. Armstrong,* four defendants in Los Angeles charged with trafficking crack cocaine filed a motion for discovery or dismissal, alleging that they were victims of "selective prosecution" by race. This motion was made after the federal public defender's office found that all 24 crack cocaine cases closed in Los Angeles in 1991 involved blacks. The district court and the circuit court upheld the motion, but the federal prosecutor refused to comply. The government then appealed to the Supreme Court, which decided in favor of the government on the grounds that the defendant did not meet the required threshold showing that similarly situated suspects of other races were not prosecuted.

In 1997, the Supreme Court rejected an appeal of a Washington, D.C. case in which an African American man who received a 10-year prison term for distribution of crack contended that the laws were racially biased in their impact. The U.S. Court of Appeals had previously rejected the challenge, stating that Congress has "not acted with a discriminatory purpose in setting greater penalties for cocaine base crimes than for powder cocaine offenses."

Conclusion

The 100:1 quantity ratio in cocaine sentencing causes low-level crack offenders to receive arbitrarily severe sentences compared to high level powder cocaine offenders. The quantity distinction has also resulted in a massive sentencing disparity by race, with African Americans receiving longer sentences than the mostly white and Hispanic powder cocaine offenders. The United States Sentencing Commission recommended revision of the 100:1 quantity ratio in 1995, finding the ratio to be unjustified by the small differences in the two forms of cocaine. Congress ignored the recommendation of the Sentencing Commission though, and refused to change the law. The President went along with the Congressional "tough on crime" stance. In April 1997, the USSC again recommended that the disparity between crack and powder cocaine be reduced, to a ratio of 5:1 by weight. It remains to be seen whether Congress or the Administration will accept this

4 *State v. Russell*, 477 N.W. 2d 886 (Minn. 1991).

more modest recommendation. Since that time, the Supreme Court has declined to find this law unconstitutional. Ultimately, public opinion will be critical to influencing public policy in this often emotional issue.

Bibliography

Edwards v. United States, No. 95–3165 (D.C. Cir. 1996). *State v. Russell*. 477 N.W. 2d886 (Minn. 1991).

United States Sentencing Commission. Special Report to Congress: Cocaine and Federal Sentencing Policy. Washington, D.C.: GPO, February 1995.

For legal positions endorsed by The Sentencing Project, see: Brief Amici Curiae in Support of the Petitioners, *Sloan v. United States*, No. 96–8145 (U.S. 1997), Amici Curiae National Legal Aid and Defender Association, National Black Police Association, et al. (11 April 1997) Brief Amici Curiae in Support of the Petitioners, *Sloan v. United States*, No. 96–8145 (U.S. 1997), Amici Curiae National Association of Criminal Defense Lawyers, The Sentencing Project, et al. (April 1997).

Where are we now with crack cocaine disparity?

Given the attention to this matter noted above and continuing to present day, many changes have been made or are pending. The Fair Sentencing Act of 2010 was an Act of Congress that was signed into federal law by U.S. President Barack Obama and it reduces the disparity between from a 100:1 weight ratio to an 18:1 weight ratio and eliminated the five-year mandatory minimum for simple possession of crack cocaine.

Developmental Theories

The get tough movement. What does this mean? In the context of the criminal justice system, it meant that during the late-1970s and into the 1980s, the US took a stance on crime called "get tough." This meant harsher penalties and more aggressive enforcement. One of the most well-known children born from this movement was the idea of three strikes laws. The most infamous three-strike policies were implemented in parts of California in the mid-1990s, and were followed by many other states and the federal system in its various forms (i.e. armed career criminal and continuing criminal enterprise sentencing); the bottom line to these harsher penalties was that anyone who was convicted of a third felony offense—most often, but not always required, a violent offense—would receive a severe punishment, ranging from twenty-five years to life.

In order to be "on board" with this type of punishment, what must you logically believe about the offender who stands subject to this type of punishment? Think. This is really important to get in order to appreciate one of the most current categories in crime theory. Developed out of lifespan sociology, developmental criminology asserts that a criminal is not born overnight. And in order to really understand crime in the hope of prevention, or at the very least in the hope of making the right decision about how we spend billions of dollars incarcerating individuals for twenty-five years to life, we need to understand that life is a series of events. In the life of a criminal, there are certain events and transitions that over time have the cumulative impact of leading the individual into a criminal lifestyle. Referred to as ***cumulative continuity*** by Robert J. Sampson and John F. Laub (1993), this term essentially notes that the events we experience in life are compounded over time by other events and will have a cumulative impact on our overall life experience—for better or for worse. This "snowball" effect, then, can help distinguish between some criminals who may just be dropping in on crime versus those who are on a clear trajectory or path of continued criminal behavior that is unlikely to cease, regardless of the intervention.

Two theories that have a user-friendly approach to understanding this developing, and at times a bit complex, category are Sampson and Laub (1993) and Terrie Moffitt's (1993) developmental theories. While these theories are quite intricate and involve in-depth research and review of many well-known cohort, longitudinal, and case studies, the key principles will be summarized so students can get a general appreciation of this category.

Sampson and Laub's Lifecourse/Developmental Theory

Summary point 1: The experiences we have in life will impact us differently depending on the timing of when they occur in our lives. For example, when I delivered the news to my ninety-one-year-old father-in-law that his closest cousin, who was like a brother to him, had passed at the age of ninety-three, it was not met with the total breakdown and utter despair that he may have felt if when he was in this thirties his cousin had lost his life.

Summary points 2 and 3: The experiences we have are impacted by historical and social contexts and also by our intimate and larger social networks. The impact of losing a sibling to an incurable disease during the turn of the century, or losing a job during the Great Depression or our most recent economic "crisis" will produce different responses and actions. Living among friends and family in your old age when learning of the passing of a loved one may be different than being a child of a single parent who is feeling isolated already when they find out a close friend has been killed in a drunk driving accident. While these examples may seem extreme, I think they make clear the points of life course theory, and that if we spent some time doing a timeline of our teen years and looked at some of the good and not-so-good turns we have taken, those turns may be connected to specific "impact" events in our historical times, the quality of our networks, our chronological age, etc.

Summary point 4: Another key principle that helps understand this life course theory is the role that choice and action play, remembering that not taking any action is action. This principle reminds us that even though one may have the greatest intent to make a positive change, change requires more than good intentions. Action is required. This principle also reminds us that actions are encouraged by opportunity or discouraged by restraints. Having the desire to go to college or settle down and have children is only as good as the financial support available. The desire to have a child of your own is contingent on having a prospective partner, or the ability to have a child alone, or adopt, and to have all the other resources necessary to take on parenthood. Desire alone is just a start. Like the non-criminal wanting to start a family but frustrated with the realities, many criminals who are on the path to a life of crime find themselves stunted as doors are shut in their faces, when a decision to act and succeed is stifled by the lack of financial, familial, and/or government support. One aspect that I think it good to note to prospective practitioners in a criminal justice or related field is to appreciate that while you may impact the lives of individuals caught up in the system, despite all your efforts and signs of change, it just might not be enough due to the life span of the individual and all the other social and psychological forces at play. When I conducted a follow-up with five of the most star pupils that I had under my supervision at a pre-release program two weeks following their release, all five residents had returned to a life of crime and/or substance abuse. For many, they had spent a year in the most nurturing, helpful, safe environment in preparation to end, or at the very least limit, their future deviant acts; however, because of the situations and the issues that they brought into the pre-release program, it was no wonder that the mission of rehabilitation went unaccomplished. As depressing as this may seem, this theory does not give up hope; it merely aims to state the obvious and what many practitioners have been frustrated with over the years, which is that intervention would be more effective if practitioners were better able to pinpoint the risk factors and, in some cases, determine who may be beyond reach.

Three terms that are very helpful in understanding, researching, and working with developmental theory are ***onset, persistence, and desistance***, which essentially ask, What makes a life of crime start? (Onset); What makes a life of crime continue? (Persistence); and finally, What makes someone decide not to maintain a criminal lifestyle before it is too late? (Desistance).

There are many factors that have turned up consistently in the research. Some of the most common explanations look at the role of human agency such as family, school experience, peer experience, and work; the role of structure, such as coming from a crime-ridden neighborhood, poverty, or a subculture; and finally, the chronological age factors. Drugs and alcohol also play a role in the lives of most criminals but are uniquely overt in the lives of career criminals.

Summary of Findings

Onset Factors

- Age—delinquent acts prior to age fourteen (NOTE: kids who use drugs before the age of fifteen are 2.5 times more likely to develop a substance abuse problem.)
- School—poor early performance, discipline issues, dropping out
- Family—having criminal family members, a large family
- Neighborhood—crime ridden, tensions with police, decay
- Peers—lack of prosocial peers

Persistence Factors

- Alcohol—alcohol abuse is never a help when trying to turn your life around. It impacts so many other critical areas of one's life and stability such as school, family, work, and intimate relationships
- Chronic unemployment
- Delinquent peers
- Peer isolation, such as being bullied, or negative peer associations such as being revered for being a bully

Desistance Factors

- Age—plays a role through development theory. Generally, most criminals desist from crime if they have not been caught up in the system, or the hands of violence, between the ages of twenty and twenty-nine. While the range is a bit long, the key is that this is not the normal lifespan of law-abiding citizens. The mid-life crisis notion, said to happen to many between the ages of forty and fifty, does not play out the same when looking at the life of a criminal and his/her criminality.

What Is It About Age?

The main premise is that the older we get, the more rational we become; in other words, the more we start to reflect upon and consider the things we may have done in the past without thinking or caring in a different light. Not all of us age the same way and at the same rate. But trying to reason with a sixteen-year-old about making a bad choice is a much more difficult task than having a discussion with someone in their twenties. While this is not written in stone and changes with individual circumstances, appreciating age as a practitioner along with some of the other factors associated with developmental criminology can provide a type of insight that is noteworthy and practitioner-worthy. In fact, many tools used for risk/need assessments note age as a critical piece of information.

Another aspect to age that is associated with desistance factors is that as we grow out of our young adult years, whether criminal or not, we start to desire a life that is more conventional, whether it be through education, marriage, starting a family, or owning our own homes and settling down. These events and experiences are all considered heavily by these theories. The application and benefit of developmental theory allows practitioners to realize that quality employment and caring about what is going on in the personal lives of those on the brink of career criminality is time worth spending. Keeping in mind the above noted principles may help a practitioner manage an offender caseload in terms of decisions and considerations for violation recommendations, outside agency referrals, level of supervision, etc.

Male and female career criminals are not exact replicas. For example, the impact of the agents of work and family often differ. Studies have shown, for example, that having a child serves as a better distance factor for women than men. Also, being involved in the military or moving away and simply starting over seems to serve men better than women.

Moffitt's Developmental Theory

A second theorist within this genre of developmental theory is Terrie Moffitt (1993). Her developmental theory notes that criminals, especially young adults and teens, can be involved in the same level of criminality, but that there are in fact two distinct types of criminals once you look beyond the criminal acts. The key point is to note that one type of juvenile is more likely to be headed for a life of crime and become a future career criminal, referred to as a life-persistent offender, while the other is simply an adolescent-limited offender and is likely to desist from crime. A small portion of the life-persistent, chronic offenders (approximately 6%) are responsible for a majority of criminal behavior. So the challenge is how to make the distinction and reduce the risk set forth by labeling theories. In sum, Moffitt has observed that these two types of criminals have different forces in their backgrounds and foregrounds that separate the two groups. I like to refer to this as "baggage." Adolescents who have more baggage, such as deep-rooted psychological problems, family dysfunction, lack of support, and anti-social personality traits are more likely to persist with their criminal and delinquent activity, while their peers who may be quite involved in criminal activity such as drug use, thefts, truancy, alcohol use, etc. seem to be doing so as part of just being a teenager. And in a society like the US where so many of the desires of young people are restricted formally and informally, they find themselves seeking those behaviors illegally in order to satisfy their somewhat natural rebellion. Moffitt refers to this as the ***maturity gap***—the gap between social and biological age. Some of the interesting, yet controversial questions that this theory poses surround reconsidering how we as a society should formally and informally respond to teen alcohol and drug use, sexual experiences, curfews, school rules on campus, etc. Recognizing how controversial and complex the issues are, using Moffitt's theory gets to the heart of why policy, practice, and theory are much more difficult to align than one might think. When I was a teenager in the 1980s, our high school had a designated smoking area, students were allowed to leave campus during lunch block, and many states allowed alcohol to be purchased at age eighteen. While this obviously would not be beneficial for some teens, and the dangers must not be ignored, this theory is suggesting that there are many teens that wish to experience and satisfy their teenage desires, and if left alone, within reason, will age out. This developmental theory provides a new kind of insight that suggests we not look at criminals in a vacuum, or incident by incident, but that we spend the time to look into background factors and current life events, with the hope of developing an assessment tool that, again, can help prevent crime; at the very least, we can be sure that if we are going to give up on someone, it is the right someone!

Activity: In small groups or on you own, consider what types of questions you would ask of an offender being considered for parole who is serving the 2nd sentence for a violent felony that reflects the insight of development theories.

Summary

While there are many emerging theories from this concept that a criminal evolves over time and that those prone to being career criminals may be identified early on as being at risk, the above theories provide a good overall appreciation for this category. These theories have also been promoted by some early theorists, such as Edwin Sutherland (1937), who focused on the criminal careers of professional thieves.

Chapter 8

Drugs and Crime

Would it be a shock to reveal that there is a relationship between drugs and crime? While it has been well established that people who use and abuse drugs, including alcohol, which is a drug, are involved in criminal behavior, the nature of the relationship is not clear. In fact, most people who use and abuse drugs and alcohol do not become hardened criminals. Aside from the "criminal" possession of illegal drugs, or possession of alcohol by minors, fortunately this behavior in and of itself is not an automatic indicator of other crimes. However, given the fact that approximately two-thirds of criminals, especially during the initial stages of their introduction to the criminal justice system (i.e. arrests, short jail time), are under the influence of "something" at the time of their offenses and/or continue to struggle with substance use and abuse following their arrests, substance abuse warrants exploration both as a contributing factor to crime in general and also as a form of crime in itself. It is also well established that teens who start using drugs early on (age fourteen or younger) are at risk for committing crimes and developing drug problems. Further, anyone who is involved in poly-substance use is at risk for developing greater drug and crime issues. This is not to suggest that waiting to smoke pot until you are eighteen will insulate you from crime or other social consequences that chronic marijuana use may bring, but it does help to appreciate the role of age, and multiple substance use, as another way to gain insight and to better predict and educate our society about crime.

Anyone who plans to or currently works in the criminal justice system or a related field is encouraged to take courses, engage in training, and keep up with literature on drug use, specifically in the physical region one works in. One of the problems in teaching and studying the relationship between drugs and crime is the fact that not all drugs are the same, and the political and social controversies surrounding certain types of drugs, such as alcohol and marijuana, make the subject matter overwhelming. For this text, and for students to come away from this course with a deeper understanding, a brief history of drugs and the various responses our society has had to drugs over the years will be discussed, followed by a more in-depth look at three models that help us understand how drug use is related to violent crime.

Drug History

Given the mass media today, one can easily access a History Channel documentary about various drugs from marijuana to ecstasy to the crystal meth epidemic. Students are encouraged to learn as much about this history and the impact and effects of the variety of mind-altering substances. However, the word of caution is to be aware that the delivery of information may be biased or impacted by certain special interest groups or agendas. Finding objective data and insight on drugs and alcohol is a daunting task.

What is a Drug?

In the simplest terms, a drug is any mind-altering substance that has an impact on the human experience. While some bring on feelings of great elation and euphoria, others may bring on feelings of excitability or relaxation. Many of the drugs used on the street today were first introduced for medical purposes to help alleviate physical pain, or to help manage mental strain and, in some cases, mental disorders. Many drugs are used and abused in combination with others for the desired effect. For example, many of the opiates that are widely used and abused today that one may receive following an operation or painful visit to the dentist, such as morphine, Percocet, or OxyContin, while different in some ways, have the common ingredient of opiate, the same chief ingredient as heroin. And even drugs that are legally prescribed to a person can become illegal if possessed by someone other than the person prescribed to. Being from Massachusetts, I am especially sensitive to the opiate problem in this area. Massachusetts is one of the leading states for incidents of opiate addiction and overdose-related deaths. In fact, for the past several years the number of deaths due to overdoses (approximately 1,500) has exceeded the number of people killed in auto accidents. And if one were to investigate other areas of the country, there are other drugs that claim the lives of individuals at different rates.

One of the reasons why drug use stakes such a claim on communities and individual lives is a combination of the power of addiction and/or the desire to seek the effect of the drug beyond its original purposes. For example, continuing to seek out a prescription painkiller long after one's physical injury is healed may be spurred by a physical need for the drug, or the need for the euphoric effect that the drug has; in other words, using something intended to address physical pain to address emotional pain or to avoid the discomfort of withdrawal.

Use, Abuse, and Addiction

One common question that arises in the discussion of drugs is what the difference is between recreational use and addiction. Simply stated, not everyone who uses drugs is destined to become what is commonly referred to as an "addict." Further, the abuse of drugs is not necessarily a sign of an addiction; however, the consequence of the abuse of a drug can be significant, both legally and physically. A good example of this is binge drinking. Are binge drinkers addicted alcoholics? While there is some controversy around the topic, there are many people, young and old, male and female, who abuse alcohol in a particular setting, whether it be at a fraternity party, a house party, or the local bar, at which time they consume many alcoholic beverages in a very short amount of time. While some intend to consume large quantities, some find themselves lured by their peers or circumstances. Binge drinking can make one more susceptible to being a victim of crime or a perpetrator of crime.

Addiction

Being addicted to a substance is characterized by physical, psychological, and social forces. One who might be facing an addiction will find themselves building a tolerance to the substance, thus experiencing cravings and withdrawal when that substance is not available. An addict often experiences psychological emotions and negative thought patterns that can significantly alter moods and behavior while under the influence or in the process of withdrawing from the substance. Another factor, which is not often discussed enough, is that social forces that indicate addiction are often significant, such as the inability to stay away from places that encourage the abuse of a substance, or subconsciously surrounding yourself with people that serve as enablers by covering up and making excuses for your substance use and/or abuse. One of the more controversial and the most common drug abused in this country aside from alcohol is marijuana. Many claim that marijuana is not addictive. However, if you look at some of the factors associated with addiction noted above, it should be easy to see how marijuana can have a physical, psychological, and social impact on a person.

U.S. Response

There have been many attempts in the United States to address drug use in our society. The five major categories are:

- **Prohibition:** a total ban on the drug.
- **Legalization:** lifting or not enacting a legal ban on the substance.
- **Decriminalization:** reducing the penalties and/or changing the criminal justice response to a substance.
- **Medicalization:** involving the medical profession in controlling and dispensing certain types of drugs.
- **Harm reduction:** looking at certain drugs and the negative impact they have and trying to find ways to reduce the harms associated with certain drugs. This may involve public awareness campaigns as well as controversial programs that try to reduce risks associated with sharing needles by providing clean needles and/or providing alternatives to certain drugs with other substances that may be less harmful.

The Importance of Understanding the Effects of Drugs

While many students have had their own experiences with drugs through their own use or observing how drugs play a role in the lives of their friends and family, having a broad appreciation of the spectrum of drugs is necessary for anyone who is going to understand some of the models and the challenges of responding to drug-related crime.

Below is a non-exhaustive list of drugs that students should be loosely familiar with in terms of their effects.

- Alcohol
- Marijuana
- Steroids
- Cocaine and crack cocaine
- Heroin (be sure to distinguish between street heroin and prescription opiates)
- Hallucinogenic mushrooms
- Crystal methamphetamines (including "ice")
- Ecstasy

Activity: Locate information on the following drugs via credible sources available on the web and/or the library that address the following questions:

What are the effects of the drug?
What forms does the drug come in and how are they most commonly used?
How expensive are these drugs to purchase?
What are some of the physical and emotional withdrawal effects of the drug?

Appreciating these questions and answers will greatly assist in understanding the final part of this chapter and the drug–crime relationship.

Goldstein's Models

The relationship between drugs and crime is well established. And the answer to the question of which came first, drugs or crime, is both. Many public order crimes such as gambling, and prostitution bring individuals into a realm where drugs are going to be more readily introduced and, in many cases, the variety of the types of drugs increased. But oftentimes, individuals who fall into the grip of addiction find themselves needing to engage in the sex trade or risk money on gambling to support a confirming habit. Property crime is another crime category that has an obvious relationship with drugs. Many addicts will resort to stealing, even from their own family members, to support an increasing habit once they are no longer able to hold down a job or the expense of use outweighs their income. In a conversation I had with an inmate (incarcerated since 1998 in the Federal Bureau of Prisons on a career criminal sentence as a repeat drug offender), he admitted that at the height of his addiction he and his girlfriend had a $2,000-a-day freebase cocaine habit. It is hard to imagine any job that would support this addiction; thus, drug dealing is also another type of crime that is associated with the use and abuse of drugs.

In order to focus on a particular aspect of the drug–crime relationship, Paul Goldstein (1985) put together three models that provide insight into the concern about the crime–drug connection in our society with emphasis on violent crime (i.e. robbery, assault, homicide). This is not to undermine or place less significance on other forms of crime, however, whether assaults, robberies, or homicides; there are far too many injuries and deaths that are directly and indirectly associated with drugs in our society.

Much of the research in support of these models focused on cocaine and heroin, but these models can be applied to just about all forms of drugs, depending on the quality, quantity, and social context. And while one could get sidetracked with how the legalization of drugs might eliminate some of the concerns the models present, that is a detour that does little to impact the reality of today or help to immediately address and reduce drug-related crime.

Three Models

Psychopharmacological

The essence of this model is that the direct effect that the drug has on brain activity can make a person violent or facilitate their own violent victimization. In other words, if the drug were not present in the system of the offender, the violence, or at least the criminal degree of violence, would not have taken place. It is well documented that alcohol is a major factor in violence, especially physical altercations that often stem from verbal arguments. UCR data reports that almost one-half of homicides are argument-invoked. And it is easy to find examples of fights that, if alcohol were removed from the environment, might not have even been started. Another drug problem that works well with this model is the abuse of steroids. This drug, and the commonly referred to "roid rage" that users experience, has been linked to some high-profile homicides. More locally, I became sadly acquainted with how steroid use and violence are connected. Several years ago, one of my students, age eighteen, was beaten into a coma by his twenty-year-old brother, who had been abusing steroids and had come home in a fit of anger and started beating his brother while he lay asleep. Thankfully, police responded in time to stop the fight. Even the boys' parents were not able to stop the beating. And while my student survived, this event has left a scar on his life, as he turned to drugs and alcohol to cope with this traumatic event. The bottom line is, he and his brother were close, and aside from the usual grumbles that occur in sibling relationships, his brother would never have wanted his own brother dead. And according to the ER doctors, death would have been a certain outcome if the police had not responded. Other drugs, such as cocaine and crystal meth, that have hallucinatory effects have also been linked to violent behavior in response to the extreme paranoia they evoke.

On the contrary, not all drugs carry the same risk under this model. For example, marijuana, especially when used by itself, is not associated with violent activity while the user is under the influence. It goes without saying that anyone dealing with drug users in the system or in their family should be aware of the violent behavior affiliated with certain drugs.

Economic-compulsive

The essence of this model suggests that drug users, either while under the influence or in a state of needing to get the drug due to the grip of their addiction, may commit a crime in order to directly obtain the drug or the money to purchase the drug. This model works best with drugs that are highly addictive. Common non-violent crimes are shoplifting and prostitution. The type of violent crime most associated with this model is robbery, which is a violent crime that involves elements of theft and the use, or threat of use, of force. UCR data indicates that almost 50% of robberies take place on the street. Many robbers use rational thinking to select victims who may be especially vulnerable due to their age, or being on the street, or the time of day, but also, many of the more amateur robbers in our society are motivated by their need to get high. These robbers tend to be more sloppy and impulsive. In some cases, this intense desire for the drug can have unintended consequences, such as a murder, when the initial violent attempt to get the drugs is thwarted by the victim. One of the most notable death row prisons in our country is Angola Prison in Louisiana. The documentary *The Farm: Life Inside Angola Prison* (1998) reveals a lot about crime, justice, and punishment issues facing our nation. One of the inmates who is interviewed and later executed was given the death penalty for the heinous stabbing of an elderly couple during an attempt to rob the couple for drug money. He was in a panicked frenzy, as he was desperately seeking cocaine. This example has elements of both the psychopharmacological model and the economic-compulsive model. This model is also one that is used as a platform for those advocating the legalization and/or decriminalization of certain drugs. The controversy is valid, and it is a dilemma that goes beyond the scope of this text. And while there are some marijuana users who may find themselves in a robbery situation in hopes of getting funds to buy some drugs, this is not nearly as commonplace as among heroin, cocaine, and meth addicts. This is where understanding the cost and availability of the drugs helps add to the proper assessment of drugs and crime.

Systemic

The essence of this model is that certain drugs, by the way that they are manufactured, distributed, and apprehended by law enforcement, create an environment that is conducive to violence. Unfortunately, recent events all across our county have illustrated how serving a warrant on suspected drug dealers can end up in horror and death. Other examples, of drive-by shootings and attempts to intimidate or get rid of witnesses after drug busts, are all too common, with more and more of these violent scenarios breaking out not just in cities, but in suburbs and rural communities. Further, as certain drug operations start to grow in size and scope, stashes of drugs and proceeds are protected with organized crime, firearms, and the willingness to engage in violence to protect the product. But again, certain drugs are better applied to the systemic model. When I was working as a federal probation officer with the Drug Enforcement Administration (DEA) and reviewing lab reports from cocaine busts, reports that the drugs were close to 100% pure said a lot about the scope and magnitude of the operation. Drugs such as cocaine, heroin, and meth that can be cut with other agents to adjust the quality in order to maximize proceeds for the dealer are especially susceptible to the systemic model. A prime example of this would be someone, addict or not, who is in the drug distribution trade who spends their money on drugs, expecting a high quality, who in turn gets duped by dealers and ripped off. Depending on the amount of money involved and/or the physical need for the customer to get high, violence may erupt once the customer finds he or she has been "punked." This model works better with some drugs than others. For example, going to a bar to get a top shelf alcoholic beverage today and being disappointed with the size or quality of the drink would hardly be resolved with a violent altercation. But during prohibition, if one were to have seen a low-grade batch of moonshine disguised as top shelf and paid for it as top shelf—this might have led to a violent confrontation. The war on drugs, which saw the crack and heroin epidemic during the 1970s and into the 1980s, was supported in part by the systemic model. And regardless of one's view on how legalization might impact the need for a consumer or distributor to resort to violence, it is simply a part of the illegal drug trade. The use of undercover agents, "snitches," and other cooperating individuals, commonly referred to as CIs, is another reality of how law enforcement can bring down large drug operations. And while a CI's name may never be revealed on a public document, any criminal who is brought down in a drug raid that stems from an ongoing investigation and surveillance operation will know exactly who that CI is once the dates of the controlled buys are revealed in the charges.

Summary

Drugs and crime are related. While most people who use drugs are not criminals, the criminal activity that stems from drugs is serious and warrants considerable attention by our criminal justice system and the larger community. Just as I was working on this chapter, the local news story was about two young adult women who had mugged a ninety-three-year-old woman in their own neighborhood in broad daylight to steal $15.00 to use to buy drugs. Both women were caught soon after and arrested on charges of robbery and assault. This class will continue to explore these models and other related issues. But even outside the context of this course, pay closer attention to reports for evidence of how these models are validated. The caution is to know that what is reported on television does not always reflect the actuality of the crime and the circumstances surrounding it in all cases. Clearly, on the day the ninety-three-year-old woman was robbed, many other individuals within her city block were the victims of violent crime. However, because of the victim's age and race and the gender and age of the perpetrators, this story captures out interest and attention. And for students who might be analyzing or developing policy and practices to reduce crime in our society, these models provide good insight into the challenges of, and the obstacles to, combating violent crime that is related to drugs.

Activity: Develop a scene that could be used in any modern-day crime show (i.e. *Law and Order, NCIS, Criminal Minds,* etc.) that illustrates each of Goldstein's models. Be creative and detailed enough that your example shows the distinctions between these three models.

Chapter 9

Putting Theory to Practice

So many of the efforts to reduce crime in our society are on the part of individuals who have professions where they have direct or indirect contact with juveniles and/or adults who are either already caught up in the system, at risk of being so, or are trying to turn their lives around. The most effective efforts are those that are rooted in theory, have been proven to work, and are implemented the way they were intended. So often, a well-intended program falls flat because those working in the agency are not well trained, or the essential things needed to successfully operate the program are not available due to budgetary restraints, overcrowded programs, and overflowing caseloads.

A *policy* is typically described as a principle or rule to guide decisions and achieve rational outcomes (Wikipedia). Putting theory into practice involves developing policies and practices that might be realized by changes of law, such as the three strikes laws or sex offender registration laws. They are also reflected in changes in how staff in an organization involved with criminals might change what they do or don't do. This last chapter provides assignments designed to help students critically think about policies and programs aimed at crime prevention, punishment, and/or attempts at reintegration and rehabilitation.

However, in addition I recommend that when viewing documentaries, films, crime news stories, or even in observing the criminal behaviors of the people in your sphere of influence that students reflect on how their responses and/or suggestions about what should be done reflect the theories taught throughout the course. It is important to remember that one does not need to take a college-level crime theory course to offer insight into criminal behavior. But being able to do so theoretically, keeping in mind social and political context and rooting insight beyond personal conventional knowledge is a skill that will no doubt add to your future and academic endeavors.

Any or all of the following assignments may be required in your course along the way for assessment and/or as part of a cumulative final course assessment. They will help you analyze, critique, and better understand the complexities and controversies surrounding crime policies and programs. These assignments may also be revised depending on individual course outcomes.

NOTE: These assignments are presented in order of the degree of difficulty.

Assignment One

Critical Thinking/Research Paper

Objectives

- To ensure that students are able to locate current scholarly/academic research information within the field of crime theory/criminology.
- To provide students with the opportunity to reflect and discuss their views on the connection between theory, a criminal behavior, and selected components of the criminal justice system.
- To provide students with an alternative form of measurement and assessment through an out-of-class writing and research assignment.

Methods

Select a form of criminal behavior (some suggestions are listed below).

- Gang-related homicide
- Mass murder (specify a type)
- Robbery (specify a type)
- Drug trafficking (specify a drug)
- Domestic terrorism
- Domestic violence (specify a form)
- Cybercrime (specify a form)
- White-collar crime (specify a type)
- Organized crime
- Hate crime
- Prostitution
- Drunk driving

Obtain scholarly/academic journal article(s) published within the past seven years that focus on the nature of the crime, its prevalence, and some of the proposed explanations.

Submit a brief paper using proper in-text citation format (MLA or APA) that addresses the following considerations/questions:

- What are some of the major contributing factors that you believe help to explain this criminal behavior in our society prior to reading the article?
- How do you believe you have come to hold your views? (i.e., mass media, job, personal experiences, etc.)

- How has reviewing the scholarly journal article impacted your understanding of why this criminal behavior occurs? (Be sure to include a brief summary of your research using proper in-text citation format.)
- Which of the three major components of the CJS (law enforcement, courts, or corrections) do you believe would be the most helpful in helping to address this crime issue and why?

Criteria for Grading
Grading will be based on covering all elements, overall presentation (formatting, in-text citation, and bibliography), clarity of summary, and the extent to which students show effort and analysis skills in their discussion. (NOTE: You may be required to submit the journal article (electronically or hard copy) along with your assignment.)

Length
Approximately 4–6 pages, double-spaced, 12 pt., typed, stapled, with bibliography.

Assignment Two

Academic Research Critique Paper

Objectives

- To ensure that students are able to locate scholarly/academic research information within the topic of applied crime theory.
- To expose students to the critical and difficult role that theory and research plays in examining criminal justice and related interventions.
- To ensure students comprehension of socio-political context and the role it plays in constructing policy and programs aimed at addressing crime.
- To provide students with insight needed to complete the program project component of this course (if applicable).

Methods
Select *three* scholarly academic journal articles aimed at a review, proposal, or discussion of any criminal justice program/policy (i.e., victim's assistance, offender reintegration, institutional corrections, substance abuse treatment, employment/educational/financial assistance, three strikes/career offender sentencing structures, drug courts, restorative justice, sex offender treatment). (NOTE: You may choose articles directly or indirectly related to the presentation component of this course.)

- Read each article and select the one that impresses you the most in terms of the realistic feasibility and positive outcomes within the program/policy.
- Submit a brief review of all three articles and a more detailed discussion about the article that impresses you the most.

- In your detailed discussion, be sure to address the following questions:
  - What makes this program/policy more appealing than the others? (Compare and contrast strengths and weaknesses.)
  - To what extent is this program/policy rooted in and/or supported by any theories? (Specify theories and explain your answer.)
  - How does appreciating the role of social and/or political context help in your assessment?

Criteria for Grading

Grading will be based on overall presentation (formatting, in-text citation, and bibliography), clarity of summary, and the extent to which students show effort and analytical skills in their discussion.

Length

Approximately 12–15 pages, double-spaced, 12 pt., with approved method for in-text citation and bibliography (MLA, APA preferred).

Assignment Three

Theory Application: Case Scenarios

Objectives

- To stress the importance of having main categories as a means to distinguish various factors used to explain criminal behavior.
- To assess students' ability to distinguish between theoretical main categories, and individual theories.
- To provide students with a variety of case scenarios depicting criminal behavior, criminal lifestyles, and those who have overcome such, as a means of practicing and/or showing expertise in their ability to use specific theories to analyze behavior.

Methods

- Select a film, documentary, or life-story account and provide an explanation for a behavior, character, and/or crime scene that reflects the specifics of any theory taught throughout the course.
- Students are also required to identify the main theory that the specific theory falls under.

Assignment Four

Program Project and Presentation

Objectives

- To allow students to work in a group or individual setting in developing a program aimed at a selected population within the criminal justice system that is based/rooted in distinct crime theories.
- To allow students the opportunity to critically assess their own ideas.
- To ensure that students fully understand the link between research, theory, policy, and application.
- To provide students the opportunity to explore a topic that is of personal and/or professional interest.
- To allow students to assess and reflect on their work through a written component.

Methods

- Select a specific target criminal population. Presentations will be designated by interest in topics so that a variety of behaviors are covered. More to be reviewed in class.
- (Examples: Certain types of homicide, assault, robbery, rape, intimate partner abuse, larceny-theft, shoplifting, embezzlement, motor vehicle theft, occupational crime (subcategory of white-collar crime), hate crime, drug dealing, public order crimes (i.e., gambling, prostitution, shoplifting, public intoxication, disorderly conduct), school violence, political crime, career offending, chronic youthful offenders, organized crime groups)
- Design a hypothetical program and/or policy aimed at addressing the criminal behavior chosen (i.e., apprehension and/or punishment, and/or correction). (NOTE: the focus of your program will depend on the selected population/criminal behavior.)
- You may use existing programs as a guide, but your program should reveal original thought and creativity.
- Your program/policy design must be rooted in three distinct criminological theories.

The following nonexhaustive list of considerations has been designed as a guide:

- Location
- Hours of operation
- Administrative order (division of labor, job descriptions)
- Number of offenders served
- Terms and conditions of participation
- Policy regarding enrollment, completion (if applicable)
- Penalties (if applicable)
- Source of funding

- Rationalization for choice of key program elements
- Political/social context considerations
- Methods for evaluation of program
- Foreseeable obstacles to success of program

Criteria for Grading

Grading for the program project and in-class presentation will cover the following:

- Overview of behavior (definitions, typologies, statistics). Feel free to use the class text to aid in this section.
- Program description (feel free to get creative and do a flyer format, PowerPoint, or poster presentation that will review the key elements, objectives, and goals of your program).
- Clear explanation of how the program/policy is rooted in three distinct criminological theories and why those theories were chosen.
- Discussion of foreseeable obstacles in the implementation of your program.
- Discussion of obstacles in completing this assignment.
- Response to questions posed by classmates and/or the professor.

Approximate Time Length of Presentation

- For groups of two to four students: 15–20 minutes. Honor system will be used with regards to division of labor. (If any issues arise with regard to participation please bring them to the professor's attention.)
- For individual presentations: 10–15 minutes.

Written Paper/Report

Everyone must turn in his/her own original report with the understanding that there will be overlap in content. The written paper should cover the following:

- Very brief overview of your program/policy (the professor may have notes from observing the presentations).
- Discussion on how the program/policy is rooted in three distinct theories and why those theories were chosen.
- Discussion of how social and/or political context might play a role in the success of your program/policy in reaching its goals.
- Discussion of how the assignment has affected your understanding of program and policy implementation in the criminal justice system.

Length

Approximately 10–12 pages, double-spaced, 12 pt., with approved method for in-text citation and bibliography (MLA, APA preferred).

References

"Policy." Wikipedia. September 21, 2018. Accessed October 02, 2018. https://en.wikipedia.org/wiki/Policy.

Appendix

Website Links to Sources of Crime Data, Programs, and Policies

http://bjs.ojp.usdoj.gov/

http://bjs.ojp.usdoj.gov/index.cfm? (NCVS, UCR, correctional data)

http://bjs.ojp.usdoj.gov/index.cfm?ty=tp&tid=3 (crime type data)

http://www.policyalmanac.org/crime/index.shtml (public crime policy site)

https://www.brennancenter.org/publication/crime-2017-preliminary-analysis (Current Data on crime trends)

http://www.crjustice.org/ (Community Resources of Justice, Massachusetts-based program) Example of community corrections programs for both the criminal adult and juvenile population as well as services for the mentally challenged.

http://www.street-soldiers.org/ (Street Soldiers—Omega Boys' Club) Documentary may or may not be used in the course. Example of non-profit organization and program with history and legacy of success.

docuwiki.net/index.php?title=The_Farm:_Life_Inside_Angola_Prison (The Farm: Life Inside Angola Prison—docuwiki.net)

http://en.wikipedia.org/wiki/Louisiana_State_Penitentiary (Angola Prison)

http://www.ussc.gov/Legal/Court_Decisions/Supreme_Court_Cases.pdf (summary of recent Supreme Court decision on fair sentencing)

http://www.sentencingproject.org/clearinghouse/ (for more detailed information on disparity in sentencing)

Bibliography

Adler, Freda. *Sisters in Crime: The Rise of the New Female Criminal*. New York: McGraw-Hill, 1975.

Agnew, Robert. "Building on the Foundation of General Strain Theory: Specifying the Types of Strain Most Likely to Lead to Crime and Delinquency." *Journal of Research in Crime and Delinquency* 38 (November 2001): 319–61.

Anderson, Elijah. *Code of the Street: Decency, Violence, and the Moral Life of the Inner City*. New York: Norton, 1999.

Benioff, Marc, and Karen Southwick. *Compassionate Capitalism: How Corporations Can Make Doing Good An Integral Part of Doing Well*. Pompton Plains, NJ: Career Press, 2004.

Brathwaite, John. *Crime, Shame, and Reintegration*. Cambridge, UK: Cambridge University Press, 1989.

Chesney-Lind, Meda. "Judicial Enforcement of the Female Sex Role: The Family Court and the Female Delinquent." *Issues in Criminology* 8 (Fall 1973): 51–69.

Cloward, Richard A., and Lloyd E. Ohlin. *Delinquency and Opportunity: A Theory of Delinquent Gangs*. New York: Free Press, 1960.

Cohen, Albert K. *Delinquent Boys: The Culture of the Gang*. New York: Free Press, 1955.

Cohen, Lawrence E., and Marcus Felson. "Social Change and Crime Rate Trends: A Routine Activity Approach." *American Sociological Review* 44 (1979): 588–608.

Coleman, James S. *Foundations of Social Theory*. Cambridge, MA: Balkans, 1990.

Cooley, Charles H. *Human Nature and the Social Order*. New York: Scribners, 1902.

Daly, Kathleen. *Gender, Crime, and Punishment*. New Haven, CT: Yale University Press, 1994.

Durkheim, Emile. *The Division of Labor in Society*. Translated by George Simpson. Glance, IL: Free Press, 1895/1933.

Goldstein, Paul J. "The Drugs/Violence Nexus: A Tripartite Conceptual Framework." *Journal of Drug Issues* 14 (1985): 493–506.

Gottfredson, Michael R., and Travis Hirschi. *A General Theory of Crime*. Stanford, CA: Stanford University Press, 1990.

Hagen, John. *Structural Criminology*. New Brunswick, NJ: Rutgers University Press, 1989.

Heimer, Karen, and Stacy De Coster. "The Gendering of Violent Delinquency." *Criminology* 37 (1999): 277–318.

Hirschi, Travis. *Causes of Delinquency*. Berkeley: University of California Press, 1969.

Homans, George Caspar. *Social Behavior: Its Elementary Forms*. London: Routledge and Kegan Paul, 1961.

Merton, Robert K. "Social Structure and Anomie." In *Social Theory and Social Structure*, 185–214. Enlarged ed. New York: Free Press, 1968.

Messerschmidt, James W. *Crime as Structured Action: Gender, Race, Class, and Crime in the Making*. Thousand Oaks, CA: Sage, 1997.

Messner, Steven F., and Richard Rosenfeld. *Crime and the American Dream. 4th ed.* Belmont, CA: Thomson Wadsworth, 2007.

Miller, Walter B. "Lower Class Culture as a Generating Milieu of Gang Delinquency." *Journal of Social Issues* 19 (1958): 5–19.

Mills, C. Wright. *The Sociological Imagination*. Oxford, UK: Oxford University Press, 1959.

Moffitt, Terrie E. "Adolescent-Limited and Life-Course Persistent Antisocial Behavior: A Developmental Taxonomy." *Psychological Review* 100 (1993): 674–701.

Packer, Herbert. "Two Models of the Criminal Process." *University of Pennsylvania Law Review* 113 (1964): 1.

Park, Robert E. "The City: Suggestions for the Investigation of Human Behavior in the City Environment." *American Journal of Sociology* 20 (1915): 577–612.

Park, Robert E., Ernest W. Burgess, and R. D. McKenzie. *The City: Suggestions for Investigation of Human Behavior in the Urban Environment*. Chicago: University of Chicago Press, 1967.

Rafter, Nicole Hahn. "Prisons for Women, 1790–1980." In *Crime and Justice*, 129–180. Vol. 5. Chicago: University of Chicago Press, 1998.

Rafter, Nicole Hahn. *Equal Treatment or Different Treatment? The Origins of Today's Policy Dilemmas in the Care of Incarcerated Women*. U.S. Department of Justice, Federal Bureau of Prisons, Female Offenders. The June 7, 1991 Forum on Issues in Corrections. Washington, DC: Federal Bureau of Prisons: 1991.

Rafter, Nicole Hahn. *Shots in the Mirror: Crime Films and Society*. 2nd ed. New York: Oxford University Press, 2006.

Reckless, Walter C. *The Crime Problem*. 5th ed. New York: Appleton-Century-Crofts, 1973.

Sampson, Robert J., and John H. Laub. *Crime in the Making: Pathways and Turning Points through Life*. Cambridge, MA: Harvard University Press, 1993.

Scheff, T. J., and S. M. Retzinger. *Emotions and Violence: Shame and Rage in Destructive Conflicts. Lexington Books Series on Social Theory*. Lexington, MA: Lexington Books/D. C. Heath, 1991.

Shaw, Clifford R., and Henry D. McKay. *Juvenile Delinquency and Urban Areas*. Rev. ed. Chicago: University of Chicago Press, 1969.

Sherman, Lawrence W. "Defiance, Deterrence, and Irrelevance: A Theory of the Criminal Sanction." *Journal of Research in Crime and Delinquency* 30 (1993): 445–468.

Stack, Jonathan, Liz Garbus, and Bill Kurtis. *The Farm: Life Inside Angola Prison*. Documentary. New York: A & E Home Video, 1998.

Stark, Rodney. "Deviant Places: A Theory of the Ecology of Crime." *Criminology* 25 (November 1987): 893–909.

Sutherland, Edwin H., and Donald Cressey, *Criminology*. 10th ed. Philadelphia: Lippincott, 1978.

Sutherland, Edwin H., Donald R. Cressey, and David F. Luckenbill. *Principles of Criminology*. 11th ed. Dix Hills, NY: General Hall, 1972.

Sutherland, Edwin H. *The Professional Thief*. Chicago: University of Chicago Press, 1937.

Sykes, Gresham M., and David Matza. "Techniques of Neutralization: A Theory of Delinquency," *American Sociological Review* 22 (December 1957): 664–70.

Tittle, Charles R. *Control Balance: Towards a General Theory of Deviance*. Boulder, CO; Westview Press, 1995.

Tittle, Charles R. "Refining Control Balance Theory." *Theoretical Criminology* 8 (2004): 395–428.

Wolfgang, Marvin, and Franco Ferocity. *The Subculture of Violence: Towards an Integrated Theory in Criminology*. Beverly Hills, CA: Sage, 1982.

www.ingramcontent.com/pod-product-compliance
Lightning Source LLC
Jackson TN
JSHW071942070825
89008JS00022B/83

* 9 7 8 1 5 1 6 5 3 2 6 3 6 *